D0667316

MEASURING BUSINESS PERFORMANCE

THE INSTITUTE OF MANPOWER STUDIES

The Institute of Manpower Studies - an independent, national centre - has close contacts with employers, trade unions, representative associations, and government departments and agencies. Operational since 1970, the Institute has become a focus of knowledge and practical experience in manpower management, the operation of labour markets, employment policy, training policy, youth training, and skills analysis. IMS expertise and resources are available to all organisations.

The work of the Institute is financed by the IMS Programme Support Fund and by income from projects. IMS subscribers work closely with the Institute at all levels, some taking the further step of joining the IMS Co-operative Research Programme (CRP) and thus helping shape the further development of the Institute. In addition to its sponsored research and its advisory work, the Institute has a growing training programme and a strong publications list.

Major IMS books and reports are published in the IMS/Gower series.

Institute of Manpower Studies

MEASURING BUSINESS PERFORMANCE

A MANAGER'S GUIDE

Judith Harper

Gower

Published by
Gower Publishing Company Limited,
Gower House, Croft Road, Aldershot, Hampshire GU11 3HR, England

and

Gower Publishing Company,
Old Post Road, Brookfield, Vermont 05036, U.S.A.

Printed and bound in Great Britain by
Biddles Ltd, King's Lynn and Guildford

British Library Cataloguing in Publication Data

Harper, Judith
Measuring business performance: a manager's guide.
(Institute of Manpower Studies series, No.7)
1. Industrial productivity---measurement
I. Title
338'.06'0287 HD56.25

ISBN 0-566-00828-9

Institute of Manpower Studies, Mantell Building,
University of Sussex, Falmer, Brighton BN1 9RF
Brighton (0273) 686751

Contents

List of Figures and Tables

List of Figures and Tables

1 Summary

This book sets out to tackle the problem of how a manager should measure the performance of the industrial unit he or she manages. It is aimed at managers, rather than their advisors or teachers, and attempts to guide, by explanation and example. No ready-made systems are presented but by the end of the book the reader should be in a position to tackle the job of establishing his own tailor-made system.

Historical Perspective

Historically performance has been measured by individual ratios, such as return on capital or output per man, and more recently value added ratios have been much in vogue. Many companies use extensive sets of ratios designed to cover every aspect of the company's business. The approach presented in this book starts from the same basis as much which is in common use today but develops a more logical and comprehensive measurement system, which is correspondingly more useful.

Systematic Use of Ratios

Since performance is the efficiency with which inputs are converted into outputs, measuring performance must involve the use of one or more ratios. Since no one ratio will satisfy the needs of all the different people interested in the performance of the firm, more than one will be necessary. But perhaps the key to successful peformance measurement is to recognise that if measures of performance are to reflect the systematic nature of the units to which they relate they, too, must be arranged in a systematic way; they must be integrated one with the other and all in turn be related to the goal of the unit.

Any attempts to set up such a system must be preceded by a clear definition of the business unit concerned and what it is in business to do, ie its objectives, output(s) and inputs. It is surprising how much disagreement discussion of this seemingly basic question can generate between managers, but also how constructive and beneficial such discussion can be.

Unit Goal

Having done this the ratios to be included in the system can be listed, including those performance measures already in use. The first ratio is obviously the goal of the unit. There will then be a productivity, price and unit cost ratio for each input factor. In addition the relationships between factors, eg capital intensity, or within factors, eg fixed to working capital, may be needed.

Having listed all the ratios thought to be needed, the system is constructed by establishing sets of equations which relate each ratio to the goal of the unit or to another ratio which, in its turn, is related to the goal. In so doing certain 'rules' are helpful and are repeatedly used in the case studies described in this book.

Problems of Defining Output

An early stumbling block in many attempts to measure performance is the difficulty of defining and/or measuring output. What is the output of a hotel, a hospital ward, a personnel department? Even the use of sales value may not adequately overcome the problem and while value added is in many ways a better measure it, too, has its disadvantages.

When physical measures are needed, standard labour hours are often used and, with the provisos mentioned in Chapter 4, this may be a suitable measure. However, it in no way tackles the problem of quality. Quality measures are essentially subjective and highly specific and hence need to be tackled on an individual basis. One of the case studies in this book does involve an attempt to measure quality which may provide ideas to other organisations on how to approach this particularly thorny problem.

Widely Varying Hierarchies

Indeed, the whole point of including case studies is to stimulate ideas rather than to solve specific problems and three very different studies are described to illustrate the widely varying hierarchies which can result in different organisations. The engineering study (Chapter 5) illustrates the use of ratios in inter-firm comparisons at a very high level of aggregation while the passenger transport study (Chapter 6) looks specifically at a divisionalised organisation and the distribution study (Chapter 7) is severely constrained by specific managerial requirements and a particularly strong adherence to certain existing measures.

Enhanced Appreciation of Business Problems

The case studies show that the ratio analysis method of measuring performance can be applied in a number of sectors and is not limited in its applicability to the manufacturing sector. They also reveal the considerable benefits to be incurred from the exercise of constructing the system, rather than from the results themselves, in terms of enhanced appreciation of the problems of the business and its true underlying relationships.

Conceptual and Technical Problems Surmountable

However, the case studies shows clearly that setting up a performance measurement system is never without its problems, be they conceptual problems of the type mentioned above concerning output, or technical problems of data collection, cost allocations, periodicity or inflation, as outlined in Chapter 9. However, it is the contention of this book that very few of the problems normally encountered in setting up a performance measurement system are insurmountable, at least in the sectors covered by the case studies and probably in many more.

Monitoring and Planning Tools

Indeed, there is little in the case studies to suggest that the methodology could not be applied in any sector, although the difficulties of dealing with very complex outputs, as found in the insurance industry for instance, or pure service units, such as R&D units, are not underestimated. Once applied, the ratio approach lends itself to use as a powerful monitoring tool and, as described in Chapter 10, a constructive planning tool either with or without the help of a simple computer model.

Thus the approach to the problem of measuring performance described in this book can provide a simple yet powerful tool to managers concerned to identify the source of poor performance in their organisation by internal or external comparisons, and to plan for improvement. The very construction of a performance measurement model can help managers understand the business which they run better and this benefit alone often justifies the effort involved. Indeed, for whichever reason the system is developed there is little doubt that the exercise will prove beneficial, in terms either of the system constructed or of the debate needed to establish it.

2 Introduction

This handbook for managers is about the performance of industrial units; it is about measurement; it is about the measurement of performance; it relates to industrial units.

First, the audience. This book is essentially a practical handbook; it is not a textbook. The author was co-author of a textbook on the same subject(1) and the theoretical basis of the approach used in this handbook was described in detail there. It is repeated here only to the extent necessary to explain the broad outline of the approach. The managers to which the book is directed need have no particular background or training. Nor need they perform any particular function within the organisation. It should be of equal interest to general management, finance, personnel and production management and whilst a thorough understanding of the unit to be measured is essential the only academic input is elementary mathematics.

Second, the contents. This book is about measurement; it is not about improvement. It gives no insight into how to improve performance, only into how to measure it. Having said that, it should be stressed that while performance can be improved without having been measured, in general the need to improve will be more readily recognised and the means to improve are more likely to be correctly diagnosed if performance has first been measured. This was certainly the case in the organisations involved in the author's empirical work on which the contents of this book are based.

Third, the subject. This book is about the measurement of performance. In its industrial context 'performance' is 'manner or success in working'(2). It is thus virtually synonymous with 'productivity', the 'efficiency of producing'(2), and is only used in preference here because the word productivity is so often not understood, misunderstood and associated only with labour inputs. The performance of an industrial unit is the efficiency with which it carries out its task of converting inputs, be they men, money, or materials, into outputs, be they goods or services. It relates input(s) to output(s).

Fourth, the scope of the technique. The measurement method described in this book can be applied at any level within the firm. 'An industrial unit' may be an entire company, a group of businesses within a company, one business within a group, a department or geographical area, a section or even an individual man, material or piece of equipment. Most of the empirical work on which the book is based has been carried out at the level of the firm or a department within a firm, ie at a fairly high level of aggregation. The greater the degree of disaggregation the more specific (and technical in the case of materials and equipment) the measures become, but the basic approach to measurement as described later is still valid.

Finally, one proviso. Every industrial unit requires its own tailor-made measurement system. Later in this book there are case studies describing such systems for a particular distribution and a particular passenger transport organisation. But this book cannot describe a system which will suit all firms in the distribution industry, or all firms in the passenger transport industry. It can only describe the way in which to go about measuring the performance of such units, guidelines to follow and pitfalls to avoid. The specific best system will depend on specific characteristics of the unit, known only to internal management. Hence this book is more akin to a 'do-it-yourself' guide than to a product catalogue.

In the remainder of this chapter the basic theory underlying the empirical work will be described and in the following chapter the general steps and rules to be applied in practice are listed. Thus Chapter 3 contains the major message of this book and should merit re-reading once the rest of the book has been read, and indeed when embarking on any new measurement exercise.

Why Measure Performance?

Before embarking on the theory of how to measure performance, however, it would perhaps be wise to consider why it should be measured. Presumably the reader has some clear idea of the answer to this question or he would not be reading the book; a desire to know **how** to measure presupposes a desire **to** measure, which is unlikely to be for the sake of the measures themselves but to fulfil some other object, most usually to improve that which is being measured. As stated above, it is possible to improve performance without measuring it but the attempt to improve is more likely to be successful given reliable measures. This is because measuring performance enables it to be monitored over time within the unit itself, or compared at any point in time with other similar units. Hence problem areas can be diagnosed and corrective action taken. All too often disagreements occur over necessary action because no agreed basis on which to analyse the problems of the business exists.

Performance may also be measured in order to provide a realistic basis from which to construct plans for the future of the unit. Measures not only indicate sources of poor performance but also constraints on performance beyond which it may be unreasonable to expect to proceed. Finally, it may be measured to provide a fair and/or agreed basis for the return to a particular input, usually labour.

Thus performance may be measured in order to diagnose problems and hence improve; in order to plan the future; or for specific purposes such as payment schemes. One basic method of measurement will suit all such objectives and in the next section of this chapter the basic theory behind this method is outlined.

How to Measure Performance

Performance is defined as the efficiency with which inputs are converted into outputs. Thus by definition a measure of performance must relate one or more inputs to one or more outputs, ie it must be a ratio. Not all ratios measure performance. A ratio of the quantity of one input used to that of another measures an input factor proportion, eg capital per man. Such a ratio describes and characterises the unit being measured, and changes in it may contribute to changes in performance but it is not itself a measure of performance. Similarly, a ratio of the quantity of one output produced to that of another measures product mix and, again, changes in it may be vital in explaining changes in performance, but it is not a measure of performance.

Thus ratios to measure performance are necessary, but all ratios do not measure performance. Neither is it possible for any one ratio to measure the performance of an industrial unit adequately. The performance of any unit will be of interest to different people for different purposes. Return on capital may be highly relevant to the shareholder and managing director but of little meaning or concern to the shop floor supervisor. Metres of pipe laid per pipe layer may be highly important to the operations manager but an unnecessary detail as far as the consumer of the product piped is concerned. Shareholders, management, employees, customers will all regard different aspects of performance as relevant to their own interests or may wish to use them for any one of the different uses outlined above. No one measure could possibly satisfy them all.

Perhaps the key to successful performance measurement, however, is to recognise that the set of ratios chosen must reflect the fact that all industrial units are systems. Inputs are not selected at random but are incorporated according to their suitability to produce the required outputs. The unit has a goal, however loosely defined, towards which all inputs (are intended to) work. If measures of performance are to reflect the systematic nature of the units to which they relate they, too, must be arranged in a systematic way; they must be integrated one with the other and all in turn be related to the goal of the unit. Thus a long list of performance measures between which the relationships have not been defined will not be of any use in improving performance, planning the future of the unit or rewarding individual inputs fairly, since it will not be possible to interpret observed changes.

It is very common when first discussing with managers how performance is measured within their company to be presented with a staggeringly (literally!) heavy tome of information, some of it in ratio form, produced on a regular, and often quite frequent basis. Honest managers admit that they only actually use a fraction of the information provided and it is rare indeed to find a document which relates any parts of the information to any other parts.

Example

Since the need for an integrated set of measures is the essence of successful performance measurement, an example may help to clarify the point. Two of the most often quoted measures of performance, at least in manufacturing industry, are return on capital and output per man. It is generally assumed to be 'good' if both these measures rise and a causal connection is often implied, ie the rise in output per man has led to the rise in return on capital. But how are return on capital and output per man related to each other?

Return on capital is profit per £ of capital employed. The equation below shows that when unit profit (ie profit per unit of output) and capital turn (ie output per £ of capital employed) are multiplied together the result is return on capital, viz.

$$\frac{\text{Profit}}{\text{Capital Employed}} = \frac{\text{Profit}}{\text{Output}} \times \frac{\text{Output}}{\text{Capital Employed}}$$

But what about output per man? Output per £ of capital employed is the result of multiplying together output per man and men per £ of capital employed, viz.

$$\frac{\text{Output}}{\text{Capital Employed}} = \frac{\text{Output}}{\text{Men}} \times \frac{\text{Men}}{\text{Capital Employed}}$$

Thus to define the relationship between return on capital and output per man involves the introduction of unit profit, capital turn and labour intensity (men per £ of capital employed).

To assume a direct causal relationship between output per man and return on capital is to ignore the relevance of these ratios. Table 1 gives a simple numerical example.

Table 1.1 : Relating Performance Measures: a Simple Numerical Example

	Year A	Year B	Year C
Return on capital	10	30	30
Capital turn	2	6	5
Unit profit	5	5	6
Output per man	2	6	2.5
Labour intensity	1	1	2

Comparing Year B with Year A, both return on capital and output per man have risen, but so has capital turn. Are the better results due to greater labour efficiency enabling more output to be obtained from the same equipment or to better equipment enabling men to be more efficient? A deeper analysis would be required to answer that question but already the simple causal link has been shown to be deficient.

Comparing Years C and A shows a more complex case in which return on capital and output per man have both risen, but so have capital turn, unit profit and labour intensity. Again, a simple casual link could overlook key contributions elsewhere.

The integrated set of ratios in the final measurement system may be expressed as a set of equations, as above, or in diagrammatic form, ie.

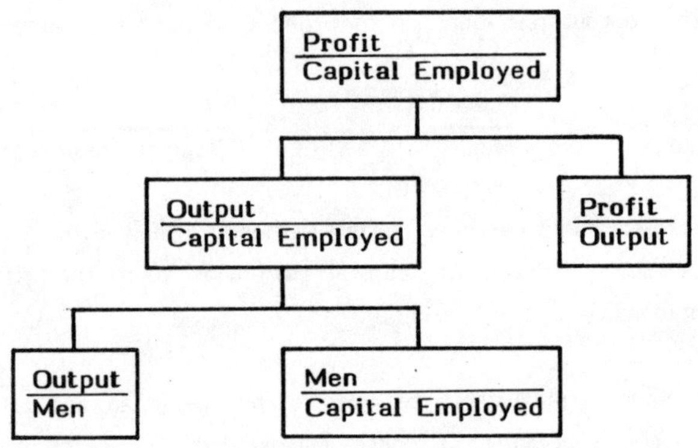

Thus to measure the performance of an industrial unit ratios are necessary, by definition. Because of the diversity of interest in any potential use of the measures, no one ratio will suffice and the set of ratios used must form an integrated whole. In the next chapter the steps to be taken and general rules to be followed for the derivation of the correct set of ratios for a given unit are described.

References

(1) Applied Productivity Analysis for Industry: Eilon, Gold and Soesan: Pergamon Press 1975

(2) Chambers Twentieth Century Dictionary

3 Performance Measurement Step by Step

In the previous chapter it was established that the measurement of performance of an industrial unit requires an integrated set of ratios. An example of a five ratio set was presented to illustrate the need for integration. Inevitably the next question to answer is: 'which ratios are appropriate?'

As stated in the previous chapter the precise set of ratios appropriate for a particular unit will be specific to that unit and as such cannot be listed here. However, in this chapter certain steps to be taken and rules to be followed are laid down to assist managers to find the correct ratios for their own units. They are summarised in a checklist at the end of this chapter and in the following chapters case studies illustrate the application of these rules in particular sectors.

Step 1 : Definition of Business

The first step in setting up the measurement system is to define clearly what the unit to be measured does. It is surprising how much disagreement discussion of this seemingly basic question can generate between managers. What is the output of the unit? How is it made? What are the key processes, inputs, market factors? How is it organised?

It may be helpful to draw a flow diagram of the organisation of the unit to illustrate the productive process and/or the areas of responsibility of different managers. It is always a problem in constructing a measurement system if areas of responsibility do not coincide with units to be measured and the flow diagram approach can highlight this problem. For instance, components for product A, along with those for other products, may be manufactured in shops B and C and assembled in shop D. All shops may have individual supervisors, but no one will be responsible for the production of product A. Yet it may be the contribution of that product which is the subject of measurement. Organisational flow charts help to clarify the precise unit to be measured and to ensure agreement on what it is that unit actually does. Figure 6.1 shows a typical such flow chart.

Step 2 : Define Unit

Having decided clearly what the unit does, it must be decided whether, in the first instance, to attempt to measure the performance of the whole unit or some part of it, one division, department, section, product, etc. If only part of the unit is to be considered, is the output of that part the output of the whole (eg a sales department), part of the output of the whole (eg a business within a diversified group) or not at all the same (eg an internal maintenance department within a manufacturing concern).

In this last case it is important nonetheless not to lose sight of the output of the organisation as a whole and this is a point which applies to service departments in general. The service is provided not for its own sake but in order to assist in the production of the ultimate output. The output of service departments must therefore always be related to that of the organisation as a whole and significant shifts in the ratio of one to the other examined.

Step 3 : Define Objective

Having decided upon the precise unit to be measured, the first major step in establishing which ratios to use is to define the terms in which the objective or goal of the unit is expressed. Commonly goals are expressed in terms of return on capital, profit margin, unit cost, or value added, but the more disaggregated the unit the more specific the goal is likely to be. However, in the case of a unit within a larger organisation care must be taken that the achievement of its goal is consistent with the achievement of the organisation's overall goal and the relationship between the two goals must therefore be clearly stated and measured. For instance, the production department may wish to raise standard hours per man; if it does so via the purchase of new equipment this may be to the detriment of the return on capital of the organisation as a whole. Even though the prime focus of measurement is the production department the relationship between standard hours per man and return on capital must be specified.

Step 4 : List Inputs

Having defined the goal of the unit the input factors used to achieve it must be listed. Normally manufacturing concerns will use men, materials, and capital while service concerns will use very few materials. It may be necessary to differentiate between grades or types of labour, components and raw materials, types of material, fixed and working capital, etc. Such categorisation will depend largely on the analysis of key processes and factors undertaken under Step 1. In the case of labour, both a volume (man-hours, days, or years) and a value (wage rate) measure will normally be needed, and in material-intensive industries the same will apply to materials. Capital will normally be expressed in financial terms only.

Summary - Steps 1 - 4

At this stage it may be helpful to summarise the first four steps in performance measurement:

1. Definition of the business, its output, major processes, organisation. Flow chart of organisational structure.

2. Definition of unit to be measured and differentiation from whole business where appropriate.

3. Definition of goal of unit to be measured and relationship to overall goal where appropriate.

4. Definition of input factors, normally labour, materials, and capital.

Before proceeding to construct a measurement system from these components one important point should be borne in mind. It is not necessary at this stage to worry too much about whether or not the factors defined can be measured in practice. The first stage is to construct the measurement system which reflects the business as it is. If it is not possible to actually measure some of the factors then either the measurement system or the data collection processes in the unit will have to be changed, but to worry about actual data at this stage may only result in sterile argument and, worse, fiddling the system to fit the available data.

Step 5 : Define Existing Measures

Collect information on measures of performance already in use within the unit. Nobody likes being presented with an entirely new system which ignores current practice, particularly if they think their current methods quite adequate. Wherever possible, existing measures should be incorporated into the measurement system; very often they will turn out to be the correct measures for the function they seek to measure and will suffer only from not being related to other measures of performance within the unit. This is particularly common in the case of standard hour measures of labour productivity, which are certainly valid in their own right but are rarely related to the overall goal of the organisation.

Having followed steps 1 - 5, a first attempt at a measurement structure can now be made. The general aim is to relate the factors defined under step 4 (and any existing measures discovered under step 5) to the overall goal defined under step 3.

Step 6 : Construct and List Ratios

a. For each input factor decide whether it is its physical quantity (eg numbers of men, tons of material) or its value (eg wage bill, material bill) or both which are of interest.

b. Relating **physical** input measures to output gives **productivity** ratios, eg output per man, output per ton of coal used. Particularly for labour, several physical input measures may be appropriate, eg men, attendance hours, paid hours. Several productivity ratios can therefore result.

c. Relating **value** input measures to output gives **unit cost** ratios, eg wages per unit of output is unit wage cost.

d. Relating **physical** input measures to **value** input measures gives factor **prices,** eg wages per man is the average wage rate, material bill per ton of material is average price per ton.

e. Relating either physical or value measures for one input to those of another gives **factor proportions,** eg capital per man.

f. Relating value input measures to the **total** value of inputs gives **cost proportions**, eg wages as a proportion of total costs.

At a greater level of disaggregation, output can be broken down by product or type or quality and **product mix** ratios constructed, eg chairs/beds, single beds/double beds, grade A/grade B. So too can inputs, giving **input allocation** ratios such as managerial to administrative staff, coal to oil.

Thus seven types of ratios can be constructed as required:

a. productivity
b. unit cost
c. price
d. factor proportion
e. cost proportion
f. product mix
g. input allocation

The 'automatic' part of the exercise is now over. Having listed all the ratios thought to be needed, the tailor-made system is constructed by establishing sets of equations which relate each ratio to the goal of the unit or to another ratio which is in turn related to the goal. To the manager inexperienced with such work the task may seem daunting but a few rules may be helpful.

Rule 1 - The More than One Factor Rule

No one factor of production can be responsible for the overall performance of the unit and the productivity of one factor can always be expressed in terms of the productivity of another factor and the proportion in which the two factors are used. Consider the following relationship:

$$\frac{\text{Output}}{\text{Men}} = \frac{\text{Output}}{\text{Capital Employed}} \times \frac{\text{Capital Employed}}{\text{Men}}$$

The productivity of labour (Output/Men) can be expressed as the productivity of capital (Output/Capital Employed) and capital intensity (Capital Employed/Men). In other words, the efficiency of the men depends on how good the capital they are given to work with is and how much of it they are each given. Relationships of this type, replacing men or capital employed by materials where appropriate, should appear in all performance measurement systems.

Rule 2 - The Pay and Productivity Rule

The cost per unit of a factor is a function of both its productivity and its price. This rule is particularly important if the performance of a unit is being measured in order to decide on an adequate rate of return to a particular factor. The following equation illustrates the rule:

$$\frac{\text{Wage Costs}}{\text{Output}} = \frac{\text{Wage Costs}}{\text{Men}} \div \frac{\text{Output}}{\text{Men}}$$

The unit cost of labour (Wage Costs/Output) is the price of labour (Wage Costs/Men) divided by its productivity (Output/Men). A similar equation can be constructed for all input factors and again such equations should appear in all performance measurement systems.

A third rule may assist in deciding which of the above ratios and equations to actually incorporate in the system.

Rule 3 - The Greatest Attention to the Greatest Proportion Rule

A useful guide as to where to start in creating a measurement structure is to examine the factor whose cost proportion is highest. A small improvement in the performance of a factor contributing a large proportion of total costs may have more impact than a big improvement from a factor contributing very little. Of course, this rule is by no means universal; the largest element of cost may be outside the direct control of the unit (for instance, its price may be administered) and there is only merit in measuring that which can be controlled.

Summary - Steps 1 - 6 and Rules 1 - 3

Perhaps the best way to summarise the above is to expand the set of example equations given in the previous chapter. For ease of reference they are repeated here:

$$\frac{\text{Profit}}{\text{Capital Employed}} = \frac{\text{Profit}}{\text{Output}} \times \frac{\text{Output}}{\text{Capital Employed}}$$

$$\frac{\text{Output}}{\text{Capital Employed}} = \frac{\text{Output}}{\text{Men}} \times \frac{\text{Men}}{\text{Capital Employed}}$$

This set defines the goal of the unit in terms of return on capital. It also involves output and two inputs (men and capital employed). In order to expand the example the third input, materials, will be introduced, as will the cost of labour (wages). It will further be assumed that a measure of labour productivity, standard hours per man, is already in use in the unit.

Steps 1 - 5 are covered by the contents of the previous paragraph, ie the goal of the unit, the inputs and existing measures. Step 6 requires a list of all the ratios to be incorporated in the system. These are assumed to be:

Profit/Capital Employed

Output/Men Wages/Men Wages/Output
Output/Capital Employed
Output/Material
Standard Hours/Men
Capital Employed/Men Materials/Men

The following set of equations incorporates all these ratios and relates them to the goal:

$$\frac{\text{Profit}}{\text{Capital Employed}} = \frac{\text{Profit}}{\text{Output}} \times \frac{\text{Output}}{\text{Capital Employed}} \quad \text{-(1)}$$

$$\frac{\text{Output}}{\text{Capital Employed}} = \frac{\text{Output}}{\text{Men}} \div \frac{\text{Capital Employed}}{\text{Men}} \quad \text{-(2)}$$

$$\frac{\text{Output}}{\text{Men}} = \frac{\text{Wages}}{\text{Men}} \div \frac{\text{Wages}}{\text{Output}} \quad \text{-(3)}$$

$$\frac{\text{Output}}{\text{Men}} = \frac{\text{Standard Hours}}{\text{Men}} \times \frac{\text{Output}}{\text{Standard Hours}} \quad \text{-(4)}$$

$$\frac{\text{Output}}{\text{Men}} = \frac{\text{Output}}{\text{Materials}} \times \frac{\text{Materials}}{\text{Men}} \quad \text{-(5)}$$

These equations are illustrated diagrammatically in figure 3.1.

Equations (2) and (5) illustrate Rule 1 while equation (3) illustrates Rule 2. The concentration of the system on an analysis of labour productivity suggests that labour constitutes the largest component of total costs, following Rule 3.

Two ratios are included in the hierarchy which were not in the original list, profit/output and output/standard hours. These are linking ratios, which may not be important in their own right but must nonetheless be meaningful. It would be **true** to say that

$$\frac{\text{Profit}}{\text{Capital Employed}} = \frac{\text{Profit}}{100} \times \frac{100}{\text{Capital Employed}}$$

but it would be a useless analysis since the ratios are meaningless. Hence Rule 4.

Figure 3.1 : Relationships Between Ratios and Goal

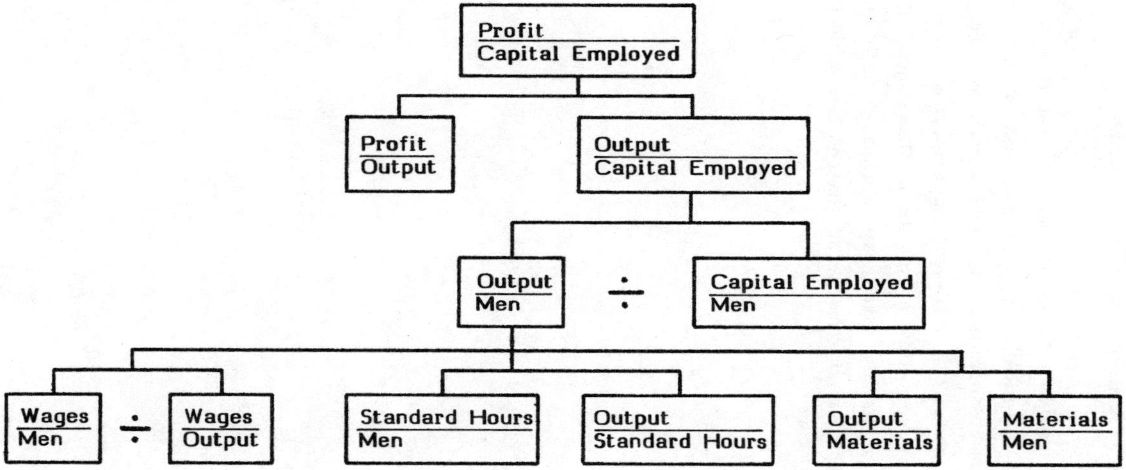

$\frac{\text{Profit}}{\text{Capital Employed}}$

$\frac{\text{Profit}}{\text{Output}}$ $\frac{\text{Output}}{\text{Capital Employed}}$

$\frac{\text{Output}}{\text{Men}}$ ÷ $\frac{\text{Capital Employed}}{\text{Men}}$

$\frac{\text{Wages}}{\text{Men}}$ ÷ $\frac{\text{Wages}}{\text{Output}}$ $\frac{\text{Standard Hours}}{\text{Men}}$ $\frac{\text{Output}}{\text{Standard Hours}}$ $\frac{\text{Output}}{\text{Materials}}$ $\frac{\text{Materials}}{\text{Men}}$

Rule 4 - Ratios Must Be Meaningful

If the incorporation of a ratio in the system involves a meaningless linking ratio it is likely that the ratio itself should not be used.

Having decided on an initial set of ratios, the next step is to collect data to measure the ratios historically; graph them; discuss the results; amend the hierarchy as necessary and repeat the process until an acceptable set of ratios for regular future analysis is achieved. However, the whole question of data collection and the presentation of results is the subject of a later chapter. Before moving on to consider some case studies in performance measurement the next chapter discusses in more detail the complex subject of how to define and measure output.

Annex to Chapter 3 : Steps and Rules Checklist

Step 1 : Define business, output, processes, organisation.

Step 2 : Define unit to be measured and output.

Step 3 : Define goal of unit.

Step 4 : Define input factors.

Step 5 : Define existing measures.

Step 6 : List required ratios

- goal
- productivities
- unit costs
- prices
- factor proportions
- cost proportions
- product mix
- input allocations

Rule 1 : More than one factor -
Productivity of A = Productivity of B x B/A

Rule 2 : Pay and Productivity -
Unit Cost of A = Pay of A ÷ Productivity of A

Rule 3 : Greatest Attention to Greatest Proportion

Rule 4 : All ratios must be meaningful.

4 Defining and Measuring Output

Many attempts to measure performance come to an early halt because of the problem of defining and measuring output. Clearly in order to measure performance, which relates inputs to outputs, measures of both are essential and while inputs are normally relatively easy to define, this is not so with outputs. For instance, what is the output of a hotel, a hospital ward, a personnel department?

It would generally be agreed that even if a satisfactory definition of output for such units could be found they would be very difficult to measure in practice. It would also generally be thought that similar problems would not arise in manufacturing industry where a tangible product is made. The difficulty of measuring outputs of an intangible nature is related primarily to the element of quality which they normally involve, although it may also be complicated by the diverse nature of the products. How can 20 meals and 50 overnight stays be summed up and the quality of service taken into account?

The problem of a non-homogeneous product applies equally to concerns producing a tangible output. A Metro is not the same as a Maestro and is not the same as a spare radiator. They cannot simply be summed to provide a volume measure of output. The element of quality is also present; a car which breaks down after 100 miles is not as good as a car that goes for 10,000; one that is delivered on time is better than one that is not etc. Hence the difficulty of measuring output with a physical embodiment should not be underestimated, although it is true that it is probably easier to define than in service organisations.

To some extent all such difficulties may disappear if the output is sold and therefore can be valued. In that case **turnover** (revenue, sales) may be regarded as a measure of output. There are, however, a number of problems associated with turnover as a measure of output:

a. Prices may be outside the control of the seller and hence changes in turnover will not reflect changes in actual output (eg government administered prices, transfer prices within a company).

b. Output may not be sold in the time period in which it is made (eg aeroplanes, power stations, ships) and hence relating the turnover in that period to the inputs in that period would give a false picture of performance.

c. Perhaps most importantly the proportion of turnover consisting of bought in materials, components or simply factored goods may vary over time and thus turnover will not reflect the work actually done by the unit. The work actually done or 'Value Added' can be simply defined as turnover less bought out materials, components, goods and services. While the ratio between turnover and work done (value added) remains steady, changes in turnover will accurately reflect changes in work done, but if a higher proportion of work is sub-contracted, for instance, a rising turnover figure can be associated with reduced internal work. (Annex 1 to this chapter explains value added in more detail).

Thus if the first two problems can be overcome and the product is sold in a free market, **value added** may be a better measure of output than turnover. It too has some disadvantages:

a. Value added may be more difficult to measure than turnover. It is not at present an audited figure and the value of bought out items may not be readily available.

b. It is in general a more difficult concept to understand than turnover and this may be important if the measures are to be used for explicative or motivational purposes.

However, neither of these measures is of use if the output is not sold in a free market and so financial measures may have to be rejected in favour of physical ones. Leaving aside for the moment the problem of quality, the major difficulty with physical measures is that of coping with non-homogenous outputs, ie how to add up x A's and y B's. In the text referred to earlier(1), an index number formulation is proposed to overcome this problem which measures the change in output from one period to the next by weighting the volume of output of each output of each product by its average price between the two periods, viz.

$$O_2 = \frac{O_{A2}\left(\frac{P_{A1} + P_{A2}}{2}\right) + O_{B2}\left(\frac{P_{B1} + P_{B2}}{2}\right)}{O_{A1}\left(\frac{P_{A1} + P_{A2}}{2}\right) + O_{B1}\left(\frac{P_{B1} + P_{B2}}{2}\right)}$$

where O: output volume, P: price and subscripts A, B, and 1, 2, refer to product types and periods respectively.

Where products are sold in a free market and where relatively few are involved, such a formulation may be useful. In practice, most organisations sell so many products that even with computer assistance it becomes exceedingly cumbersome. More importantly, the need for physical measures is paramount when there is **no** free market price available.

Another way of overcoming the summing problem may be to reduce non-homogeneous outputs to a number of common factors. In its simple form this involves taking a base product and denominating all other products in terms of that one, eg product B = 1.5 x product A. The basis of such a procedure is normally the standard manpower input to each product, ie the above implies that it ought to take 1.5 times the man-hours to produce B as A. Summing all the A's and B's produced in this way is therefore equivalent to summing standard man-hours.

As a measure of output this has three major problems:

a. It requires measures of standard man-hours which may not be available because the product does not lend itself to such measurement, eg it is non-repetitive.

b. Such measures are at least to some degree subjective and capable of manipulation.

c. It assumes that the contribution of the other input factors (especially capital and materials) is equal per standard labour hour. Using the example above, 1 x A + 1 x B = 2.5 units of output. But considerably more material and capital may be associated with each standard man-hour that goes into A than into B. Summing standard units of one input ignores such inequalities.

This last problem could be overcome if standard values were also available for any other inputs used. If the totals of all standards can then be expressed in common units and summed, a measure of output is available, (although problem b) above would still exist. An example of this procedure is given in Annex 2 to this chapter.

None of these methods, however, overcome the problem of measuring quality and, since quality measures are essentially subjective and highly specific, this is not a problem that can be solved in a general book such as this. It is tackled in one of the case studies later in the book and the approach taken in that organisation could be generalised. It remains the case, however, that, particularly in the service sector and to some extent within manufacturing, the definition and measurement of output is often the most difficult part of setting up adequate performance measures.

This chapter has been included rather to reassure the reader that the problems of output definition and measurement are real ones and are recognised as such, than to solve them. Those who consider the hurdle of output measurement insurmountable should not be deterred from reading on, however. The case studies which follow may generate ideas from which solutions will evolve and assist in the clear thinking about the exact nature of the business which is so essential before the problem of output measurement can even be tackled.

Annex 1 to Chapter 4 : Value Added

'Value Added' is the value which the firm adds to the materials, components, goods and services which it buys from other firms to create its own turnover or sales revenue. It can be calculated in two ways:

Subtractive Method

Value Added = Turnover - Value of Bought Out Items, ie Materials,
Components, Goods, Services.

However, Turnover = Bought Out Items + Wages + Depreciation + Profit. Hence

Addititive Method

Value Added = Wages + Depreciation + Profits

Annex 2 to Chapter 4 : Output Measurement Example

Number of Units Output

	Period 1	Period 2
Product A	100	90
Product B	20	40

Standard Labour Content (Hours)

Product A	600
Product B	800

Standard Material Content (£)

Product A	400	(600)*
Product B	800	

Labour and Material Content of Actual Output

	Labour (hours)	Materials (£)
Period 1	600 x 100 = 60,000	400 x 100 = 40,000 (60,000)
	800 x 20 = 16,000	800 x 20 = 16,000
	76,000	56,000 (76,000)
Period 2	600 x 90 = 54,000	400 x 90 = 36,000 (54,000)
	800 x 40 = 32,000	800 x 40 = 32,000
	86,000	68,000 (86,000)

Output Measure (Valuing Labour at £2 per hour)

	Period 1	Period 2	% Change
Labour	152,000	172,000	+13.2
Materials	56,000(76,000)	68,000(86,000)	+21.4(+13.2)
Total	208,000(228,000)	240,000(258,000)	+15.4(+13.2)

Thus the change in output (+15.4%) is a weighted average of the changes in standard labour hours (+13.2%) and material content (+21.4%). If material content **were** constant per standard labour hour then the bracketed figures would apply and changes in standard labour hours would reflect changes in output.

* if material content standard per labour hour

5 Engineering — Case Study I

This first case study describes the initial empirical work carried out by the author, in conjunction with the Engineering Employers' Federation and the Institute of Manpower Studies, to test the practical relevance of the ratio approach to performance measurement. Its objective was to construct a set of ratios which would be appropriate in the 'average' batch-production engineering company, and which such a company could then use as a base from which to proceed to its own tailor-made system.

The manpower resources available to carry out the study limited it to 20 companies and with such a relatively small sample it was essential to cover as limited a range of products and manufacturing processes as possible. The machine tool sector was selected as it was regarded as representative of much of the engineering industry, given the predominance of batch-production methods.

The 20 firms participating in the study ranged in size from 55 to 2600 employees and £500,000 to £27 million turnover on average over the period 1973-1977. Together they accounted for approximately 10 per cent of all establishments in the sector employing 50 or more people and 20 per cent of the turnover. A reasonable size and geographical spread were achieved.

The study was conducted in three stages. The first was statistical; for each of their last five financial years the firms were asked to complete a detailed questionnaire about their organisation included in Annex 1 to this chapter. From this information a very large number of ratios, illustrated in figure 5.1, were calculated. The information also provided an insight into non-financial aspects of the organisation, for example changing product mix, market trends, employment structure and operating constraints, in advance of the second stage of the study.

Figure 5.1 : The Complete Engineering Hierarchy

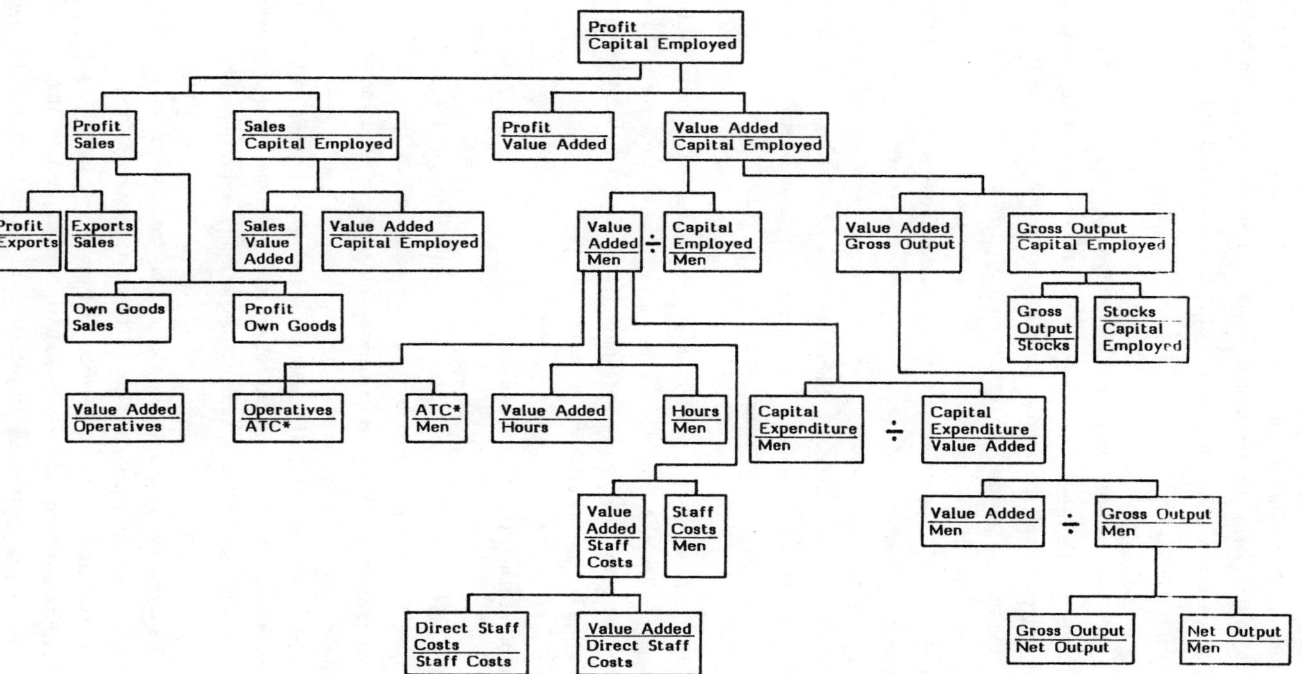

*ATC : Administration, Technical and Clerical Staff

The second stage consisted of fieldwork discussions. With the benefit of information already supplied in the questionnaires the project team spent a whole day with each firm in discussions with managers and trade union representatives; on average, five separate interviews were held at each establishment.

The third stage of the project consisted of analysis of the data and the information gathered in interviews. One objective at this stage was to compare and contrast the attributes of the more successful firms with those of the less successful, and thereby to establish which set of ratios 'explained' the differences between them. If the performance of one company is measured over a number of years then the 'right' set of ratios should explain why performance levels have changed. Similarly, if several companies involved in the same business are examined in the same year the 'right' set should explain differences in performance between them. In this case study, four firms performed significantly better than the remainder and therefore their characteristics were compared with those of the less successful group.

Obviously, for the purposes of this book it is not the numerical results of the exercise which are of interest but the set of ratios chosen. However some of the results are given graphical form in figure 8.6 in Chapter 8, since they illustrate one way in which results can be presented.

Performance Indicators : The Complete Set

The questionnaire set out to gather information to construct the hierarchy illustrated in figure 5.1. The hierarchy looks cumbersome largely because in the first instance the project team was uncertain which measure of output to use. Since the machines were sold in a free market there was no need to avoid financial measures and a physical measure would in any case have been impossible to construct. However, various alternative financial measures were considered, in particular Sales, Gross Output, Net Output, and Value Added.

The difference between Sales and Gross Output is the change in stocks of finished goods and work in progress. The difference between Gross and Net Output is bought out items. The difference between Net Output and Value Added is such items as non-industrial services, motor vehicle licences and rates. Clearly the biggest difference is between the 'Gross' concept of Sales and Gross Output and the 'Net' concept of Net Output and Value Added; whether to use the Gross or Net concept depends largely on whether the ratio between the two varies significantly between firms or over time. Clearly, in a sector like machine tools it does and therefore Net Output or Value Added gives a fairer reflection of what the company actually produces itself, rather than Gross Output or Sales. Within one company, if the ratio is fairly stable over time, sales and value added would be interchangeable as measures of output. In this case all ratios involving Gross and Net Output were discarded and two sales ratios were retained since they were in common use in the industry.

Analyses of sales into own goods and/or exports did not appear to assist in explaining the better performance of some firms and neither did the breakdown of the labour force into operatives, administration, technical and clerical staff. Data on man-hours, direct payroll costs and capital expenditure were not always readily available. Hence a sub-set of ratios remained, illustrated in figure 5.2, for which data were available, which used an agreed measure of output, and which did all appear to contribute to explaining the superior performance of some companies. How they were calculated from the information on the questionnaire is shown in Annex 2 to this chapter.

Figure 5.2 : Key Ratio Engineering Hierarchy

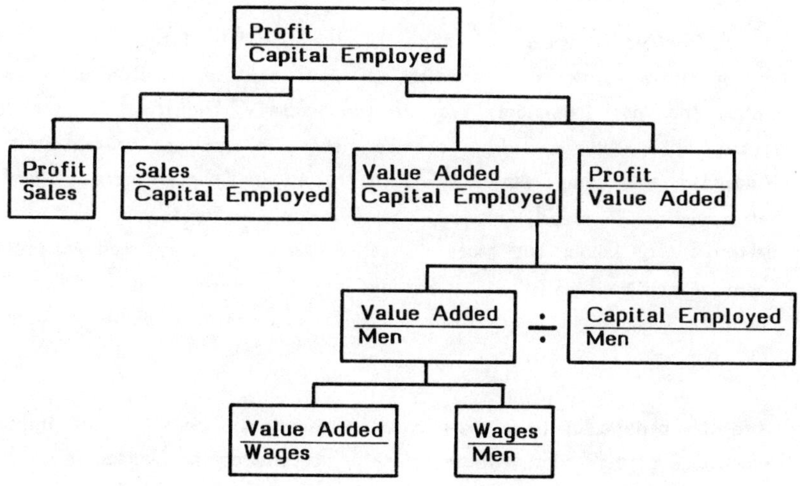

Performance Indicators - The Key Set

The key set of ratios was:

- o Return on capital (Profit/Capital Employed)
- o Profit Margin (Profit/Sales)
- o Capital Turn (Sales/Capital Employed)
- o Share of Profit in Value Added (Profit/Value Added)
- o Capital Productivity (Value Added/Capital Employed)
- o Labour Productivity (Value Added/Men)
- o Capital Intensity (Capital Employed/Men)
- o Value Added per £ Payroll Costs (Value Added/Wages)

Clearly the average wage rate (Wages/Men) is also required to link labour productivity and Value Added per £ of wages, but it was not a key ratio in terms of explaining differences between firms.

Value Added per £ of wages is, of course, also interesting in its inverse form since the share of wages in value added can be a useful starter for a value added incentive scheme, the objective of which is to reduce that proportion and hence leave more for profit.

Having decided on return on capital as the objective of the organisations, this set of ratios breaks it down first to show the contribution of sales-based ratios, the most commonly used in the industry, and then, for the reasons stated above, value added-based ratios. These in turn are broken down using Rules 1 and 2 from Chapter 3. As the results in Chapter 8 show, these eight ratios distinguish clearly between better and poorer performers and show how better use of labour and more capital per man are associated with a higher share of profit in value added and hence a higher return on capital. How to calculate these eight ratios from actual data is shown in detail in Annex 2 to this chapter.

With the benefit of later experience, however, and perhaps more importantly experience of constructing hierarchies for specific companies and using them to explain specific changes in performance levels, this hierarchy can be seen to be defective. Most importantly, it breaks down that element of return on capital which does **not** explain differences between companies (Value Added/Capital Employed) rather than the one that does (Profit/Value Added). On average, profit contributed 33 per cent of the value added of the best firms, whilst for the sample as a whole the figure was under 20 per cent. Meanwhile the ratio of value added to capital employed was actually lower for the better firms than for the sample as a whole. This was due to relatively high capital employed in the best firms but nonetheless a truly explanatory hierarchy would have analysed profit/value added rather than value added/capital employed.

This could be done simply by using the equation

$$\frac{\text{Profit}}{\text{Value Added}} = \frac{\text{Profit}}{\text{Men}} \div \frac{\text{Value Added}}{\text{Men}}$$

and then breaking down Value Added/Men as before, and into Value Added/Capital Employed and Capital Employed/Men, using Rule 1, giving the hierarchy illustrated in figure 5.3. An alternative would be to use the equation

$$\frac{\text{Profit}}{\text{Value Added}} = \frac{\text{Profit}}{\text{Wages}} \times \frac{\text{Wages}}{\text{Value Added}}$$

It would then be necessary to break down the latter using Rule 2 into Wages/Men and Value Added/Men, and to break down Value Added/Men using Rule 1 as in figure 5.3, giving the hierarchy shown in figure 5.4.

The only way to choose between these alternatives is to see empirically which gives the most sensible results and thus commences the iterative process which is a key part of successful performance measurement. Hierarchies are suggested, tested, rejected or amended and re-tested until a satisfactory explanation of past differences or changes is reached.

Conclusion

This case study has been included in order to illustrate the way in which a hierarchy might be developed rather than to present a hierarchy which is considered suitable for an engineering firm. Nonetheless the sets of ratios presented in figures 5.2-5.4 could provide a good starting point for a manufacturing company, especially one involved in batch production, from which a set more specifically designed to meet individual requirements could be derived.

Figure 5.3 : Revised Key Ratio Hierarchy

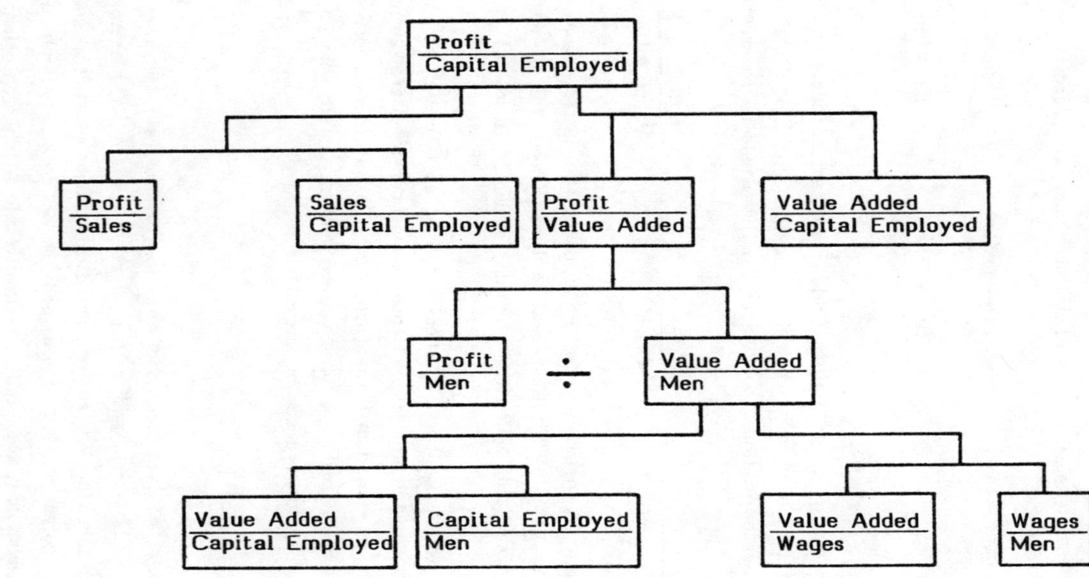

Figure 5.4 : Alternative Revised Key Ratio Hierarchy

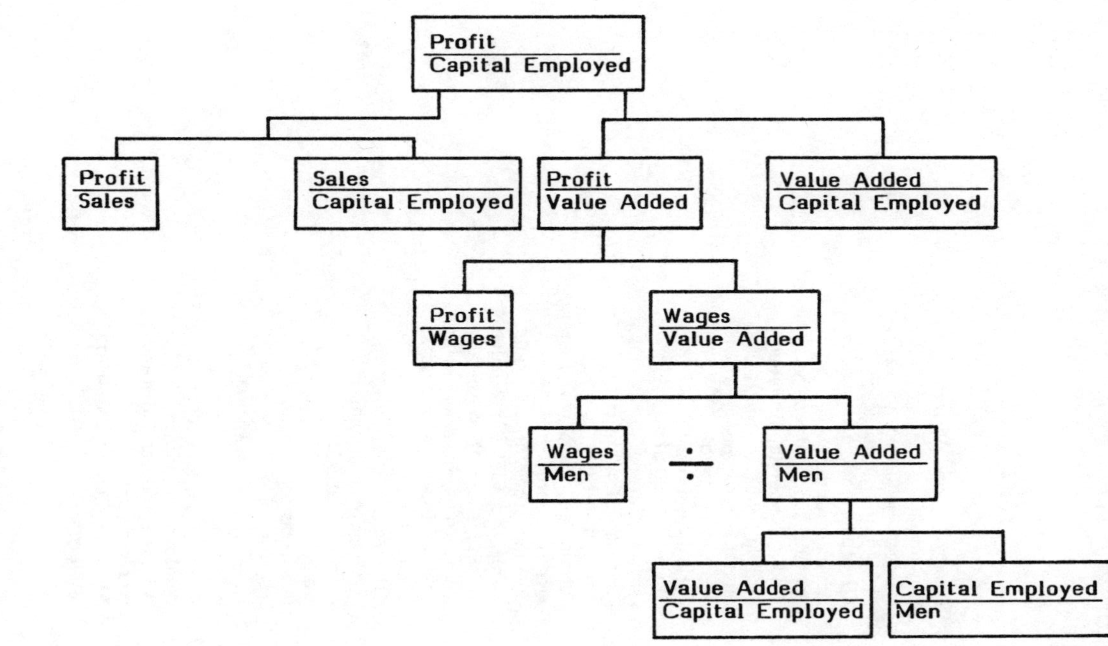

Annex 1 to Chapter 5 : Engineering Questionnaire

All financial data should be provided exclusive of VAT and uncorrected for inflation. Some sample results for year 5 have been included as examples.

Item No.		Year 1	Year 2	Year 3	Year 4	Year 5	Item No.
		( )	( )	( )	( )	(1977)	
1	Sales of goods of own production					14,000	1
2	Sales of goods bought & sold without reprocessing					600	2
3	All other work done and services rendered					150	3
4	Opening stock of goods on hand for sale (book value)					650	4
5	Closing stock of goods on hand for sale (book value)					600	5
6	Opening stock of work-in-progress (book value)					3,000	6
7	Closing stock of work-in-progress (book value)					4,000	7
8	Purchase of materials, stores and fuels					4,700	8
9	Purchase of goods for re-sale without reprocessing					450	9
10	Opening stock of materials, stores and fuel (book value)					300	10
11	Closing stock of materials, stores and fuel (book value)					500	11
12	Cost of industrial services received					300	12
13	Other costs (non-industrial services, motor vehicle licences, rates)					800	13
14	Wages					5,700	14
15	Profit before tax and interest					2,300	15
16	Average net fixed assets employed					1,900	16
17	Average working capital employed					6,800	17
18	Average number full-time employees					1,400	18
19	Average number part-time employees					30	19

Explanatory Notes

Item No.		Census Code
1	At nett selling value (ie less discounts, commissions etc)	L261
2	ie goods merchanted or factored	L266
3	Includes: receipts for work done and industrial services rendered; work of a capital nature carried out by own staff; receipts for non-industrial services rendered	L262 L252 L267
4	At 'sales' value	G3 Cols B or
5	At 'sales' value	G3 C or sum
6	At 'sales' value	G2 of both
7	At 'sales' value	G2 where appropriate
8	Raw materials, components, fuel etc	K734
9		K733
10		G1 Cols. B or
11		G1 C or sum of both
12	Amounts paid to other firms for sub-contracts, repairs, etc	J623
13	Hire of plant etc; rent; insurance premiums paid, bank charges; other services	J2
	Motor vehicle licences	O276
	Rates	O277
14	Gross wages and salaries paid to employees, remuneration of outworkers, and employers' NI/earnings related contributions to other pension and welfare schemes	Section F
15	As in company profit and loss account, including profit plus interest payable less share of profits of associated companies.	
16	As in the company balance sheet; net book value of land, buildings, vehicles, plant machinery and other capital equipment	
17	Includes inventories, debtors less trade creditors/accruals, but excludes sources of finance eg overdrafts, loans, etc.	

Annex 2 to Chapter 5 : Calculation of Ratios

1 This annex shows how the data supplied in the Questionnaire in Annex 1 can be used to calculate the key ratios described in Chapter 5.

2 In order to calculate the deflated ratios (Capital Employed/Men and Value Added/Men) the price deflators in Table A1 were used:

Table A1 : Price Deflators*

Financial year end	1973	1974	1975	1976	1977	1978
January	-	1.28	1.52	1.91	2.20	2.49
February, March, April	-	1.33	1.61	2.00	2.27	2.55
May, June, July	1.22	1.39	1.71	2.07	2.35	-
August, September, October	1.25	1.45	1.81	2.14	2.43	-
November, December	1.28	1.52	1.91	2.20	2.49	-

3 The deflator most appropriate for the specific financial year-end should be used. If the year-end is in March the figures in Lines 11 and 15 of the Analysis Form should be divided by those in the second line of Table A1; if it is in June by those in the third line etc.

4 This method of deflation does not remove stock appreciation profits, ie those profits arising from an increase in the value of stocks held by the company. These are very significant in periods of high inflation and as a consequence value added figures deflated as above are overstated in such periods.

* These are the deflators used by the Central Statistical Office to convert the total expenditure of all goods and services in the UK to constant 1970 prices.

Analysis Form

	Instructions	Year 1 ( )	Year 2 ( )	Year 3 ( )	Year 4 ( )	Year 5 (1977)	
1	S = Sales, Item Nos 1+2+3					14750	1
2	Add Item Nos. 5+7					4600	2
3	Add Item Nos. 4+6					3650	3
4	Subtract line (3) from line (2)					950	4
5	Gross Output, line (1) + line (4)					15700	5
6	Item No. 11					500	6
7	Add Item Nos 8+9+10+12					5750	7
8	Subtract line (7) from line (6)					(5250)	8
9	Net Output, line (5) + line (8)					10450	9
10	Item No. 13					800	10
11	Value Added, line (9)-line (10)					9650	11
11a	Value Added (deflated) - see paragraphs 2/3					4386	11a
12	Men Item Nos. 18+(19/2)					1415	12
13	Wages Item 14					5700	13
14	Profit Item 15					2300	14
15	Capital Employed, Items 16+17					8700	15
15a	Capital Employed (deflated - see paragraphs 2/3)					3955	15a
16	Return on Capital (line (14) ÷ line (15)) x 100					26%	16
17	Profit Margin (line (14) ÷ line (1)) x 100					16%	17
18	Sales/Capital Employed, line (1) ÷ line (15)					£1.70	18
19	Profit/Value Added (line (14) ÷ line (11)) x 100					24%	19
20	Value Added/Capital Employed, (line (11) ÷ line (15))					£1.11	20
21	Value Added/Men (line (11a) ÷ (12)) x 1000					£3100	21
22	Capital Employed/Men (line (15a) ÷ line (12)) x 1000					£2800	22
23	Value Added/Wages (line (11) ÷ line (13))					£1.69	23
24	Wages/Value Added (1 ÷ line (23)) x 100					59%	24

6 Passenger Transport — Case Study II

This chapter describes the application of the ratio hierarchy method of performance measurement in an organisation providing a passenger transport service. The project arose as a result of the organisation's desire to improve its performance and to be seen by its employees and passengers to be trying to do so. Some of the lessons learnt are specific to the organisation alone and these will not be explored in this chapter. Some are applicable to organisations in a similar business. Many are generally applicable, particularly the extension of the set of ratios to measure the performance of a divisionalised and/or functionally organised operation. The results of the project were an invaluable aid to the organisation in presenting information concerning itself to an official examining authority.

Distinguishing Features of the Organisation

The organisation transports passengers by bus to and from a large number of pick-up points. It is publicly owned and does not determine its own fare structure. Its output cannot therefore be fairly measured in terms of revenue nor can it realistically work to revenue or profit objectives.

It is organised in a number of departments (figure 6.1). The Operations Department runs the Garages, which maintain the buses on a day-to-day basis, and Bus Operating which is supplied with buses by the Garages and runs them. The Engineering Department carries out major overhauls of buses at one works and routine maintenance and repairs at another. Both the Engineering Department and the Garages draw supplies from the Main Stores. Figure 6.1 is an example of the type of flowchart referred to above (Chapter 3) which can clarify the precise nature of the output of the business as a whole and of individual parts of it.

The important performance measurement feature of the structure illustrated by figure 6.1 is that only the Operating Department produces the output of the organisation as a whole. The other departments provide a service to Operating, or to each other - a service which cannot be valued (although it can to some extent be costed).

Figure 6.1 : Passenger Transport Organisation Flow-Chart

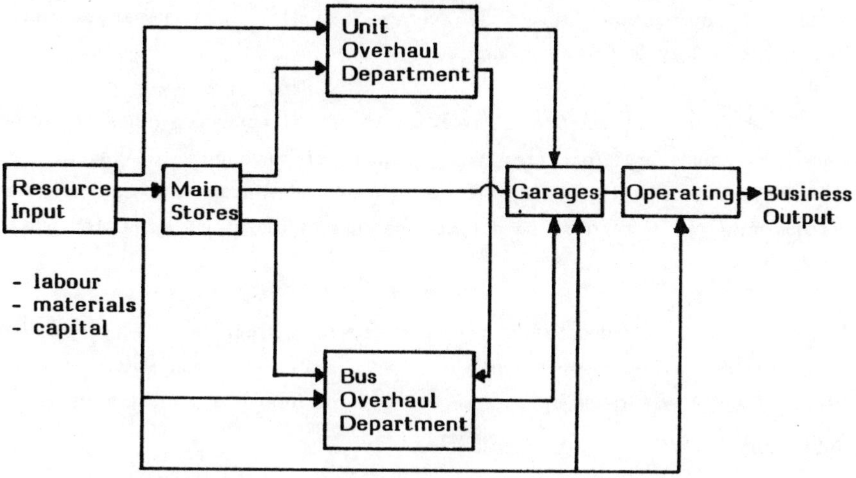

Unit Overhaul Department

Resource Input

- labour
- materials
- capital

Main Stores

Garages

Operating

Business Output

Bus Overhaul Department

These two features of the organisation - the lack of control over prices and the functional structure - create two problems when it comes to measuring performance. The first and most obvious is the measurement of output. The second, and most interesting in terms of the general application of this work, is the establishment of linked sets of ratios for departments which do not produce the ultimate output. In the next section the method of tackling these fairly common problems adopted in this particular case is described.

Measurement of Output

As has already been stated, the organisation's lack of control over the fare structure prevents the use of any financial measure of output for the purposes of measuring performance. However, three volume measures of output are available: bus miles (the total number of miles run by all buses); place miles (the total number of miles run by all passenger places (whether seated or standing, occupied or not) on all buses); and passenger miles (the total number of miles travelled by passengers). Of these three, bus miles and place miles are simple volume measures (linked by average bus size) while passenger miles incorporate quality and price influences.

It may at first sight seem most relevant to regard passenger miles as output since they could vary from zero to the number of place miles. However, since the fare structure will obviously be a significant determinant of passenger miles per bus mile, the latter may be a fairer measure of the output generated within the business.

It was eventually decided to use both measures of output but to recognise that they measured different aspects of the organisation's operations. Passenger miles per £ of costs was taken to represent overall performance while bus miles per £ of costs measured internal efficiency.

Before completing the discussion of output measurement the connection between these two measures should be considered. The linkage must be clearly defined or it will not be clear whether an improvement in internal efficiency has been beneficial in terms of overall performance. One link is average bus size (place miles per bus mile). Another is the level of fares, as stated above, and another the quality of the bus miles offered. Were the buses on time, comfortable, clean? Whilst no measures of cleanliness or comfort were available the organisation did measure 'average waiting time', ie the average time spent waiting at the bus stop.

On high frequency routes, where timetables are not published and passengers can be assumed to arrive at bus stops at random (85 per cent of the routes provided), average waiting time can be used as a measure of the quality of the bus service. The problem then is to link passenger miles per £ of costs with bus miles per £ of costs using average bus size (place miles per bus) and average waiting time. Before discussing this problem, however, the discussion of output measurement must be completed.

Bus miles can only be regarded as the output of the organisation as a whole and of the Operating Department. The service departments shown in figure 6.1 are crucial to the Operating Department's ability to produce bus miles but are themselves responsible for quite different outputs: consumable materials, overhauled and repaired units, overhauled buses and buses ready for service.

At first glance a volume measure of output for these departments might appear quite easy to achieve; volume of materials, number of units overhauled or repair, number of buses overhauled or made ready for service. However, since there is a very great variety of units involved and also various bus types and indeed overhaul types, the problem is in fact quite complex. No value is placed on the output from or indeed the input to these departments and so there is no immediately available weighting mechanism. Some steps have been taken since the author's involvement with the organisation to establish more accurate cost information, and the need to decide appropriate market prices is now being taken very seriously.

In the absence of this information the method of measuring output described in Annex 2 to Chapter 4 could have been applicable but in the Unit Overhaul and Repair Department another method was in fact used. Major items were put out to competitive tender outside the company and the lowest estimate received was taken as the 'standard' value of the work. The values were then summed over all those items actually repaired and the total grossed up to allow for the small (15) percentage of items not included in the exercise. This could then be regarded as 'output' and compared with the actual costs of carrying out the work.

Clearly, the establishment of the standard costs could be a lengthy exercise and it would rarely be worthwhile to carry it out simply in order to measure output; in this case it had been done before the performance measurement exercise was undertaken, in order to establish the improvement in productivity which could be achieved were the organisation to be competitive with the outside market. There are also many arguments to say that it is not a totally just measure of output, but the strength of these will depend on the precise nature of the work undertaken and of the facilities used. However, it is an approach to the problem of summing diverse physical outputs which are not valued within the company which could possibly be adapted in the reader's particular case and therefore should be borne in mind.

Before passing from the subject of output measurement it is relevant to quote the case of another organisation involved in passenger transport but in this case by rail, particularly because of the light it throws on the measurement of the qualitative element of output. Many of the output measurement problems in this case were similar to the bus business but a major distinguishing feature was the existence of a department responsible for laying new, and maintaining and repairing existing, track. Clearly the total volume of track would be known in each period but would vary very little from period to period and changes in it would not reflect the output of the department, whose efforts are directed primarily to maintaining or renewing existing track. Thus the quality of the track is involved and the measure required is in fact 'miles of track of a certain quality'. In this particular case, the department had inspectors who 'marked' each length of track on a regular basis and thus the total length of track could be adjusted by the composite mark to give a more relevant measure of output.

As in the case of non-valued diverse physical outputs described above, a time-consuming exercise would have to be undertaken to construct such a measure; in this case it had been necessary anyway to ensure the safe running of the trains. It is in fact probably true that if outputs are not valued in a free market, and/or if they contain a significant quality element, their measurement will be relatively subjective and possibly time consuming. This is not to say that the results will not repay the efforts involved.

Performance Indicators : Overall Performance

Returning to the bus case study and the linkage between overall performance and internal performance, via average bus size and average waiting time, figure 6.2 introduces the concept of Bus Service Units defined as Place Miles per Minute of Average Waiting Time. The Bus Service Unit is a measure which attempts to take into account both the quantity (place miles) and quality (average waiting time) of output. It may be interpreted as the amount of what the customer really wants provided.

Overall performance, passenger miles per £ of cost, is thus broken down into Bus Service Units per £ of costs and Passenger Miles per Bus Service Unit - the amount of the service offered actually used. The latter will of course be principally determined by fares and is therefore not analyised further; there is little point in detailed analysis of ratios outside the control of the organisation.

Figure 6.2 : Overall and Internal Performance Hierachy

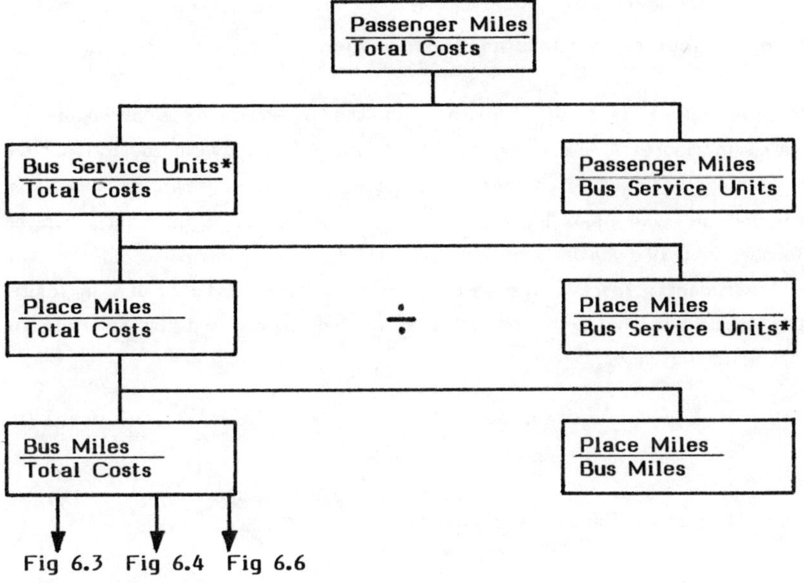

* Bus Service Units = $\frac{\text{Place Miles}}{\text{Average Waiting Time}}$

Bus Service Units per £ of costs can, however, be broken down into it quantity and quality elements, place miles per £ of costs and place miles per bus service unit. Since bus service units are place miles per minute of average waiting time, place miles per bus service unit is simply average waiting time. Place miles per £ of cost can then be broken down into internal performance (bus miles per £ of costs) and average bus size, and thus overall performance and internal performance are linked.

Such a hierarchy is clearly relevant to any passenger transport organisation in which the data are available and could be adapted to suit organisations distributing goods rather than passengers. Its exact nature was arrived at by the repetitive process described earlier; ratios to be included were listed, equations set up and evaluated, the results discussed and the equations altered until a meaningful set was reached. A similar process was applied to break down internal performance.

Performance Indicators : Internal Performance

Three alternative sets of indicators for the organisation as a whole are illustrated in figures 6.3, 6.4 and 6.6. In figure 6.3 the overall objective, the maximisation of bus miles per £ of cost, is broken down to show the contribution of each major input category in cost terms, ie materials, capital and labour; in figure 6.4 it is broken down to show the contribution of the two major departments (Operations and Engineering) and overheads; finally, in figure 6.6 the breakdown shows the contribution of the Budget and the Schedule to internal efficiency.

Figure 6.3 : Input Factor Analysis

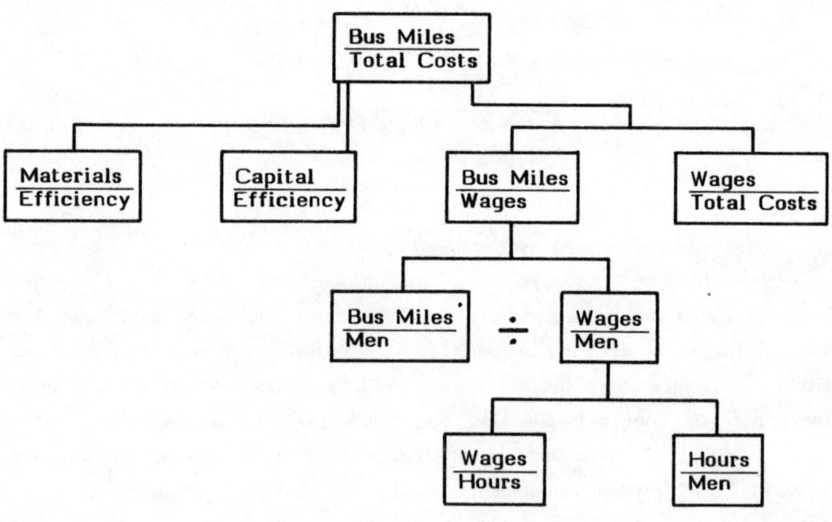

Input Approach

In figure 6.3 the initial breakdown of bus miles per £ of cost follows Rule 3 from Chapter 3 by identifying the major cost proportion(s), using the identity:

$$\frac{\text{Bus Miles}}{\text{Cost}} = \frac{\text{Bus Miles}}{\text{Wages}} \times \frac{\text{Wages}}{\text{Cost}}$$

where material costs and capital costs can be substituted for wages. Wages divided by cost is the input cost proportion (in this case wages) while bus miles per £ of wage cost is the contribution of the cost category to output - the inverse of unit cost.

In the relatively short term cost proportions tend to remain fairly steady; they are therefore not analysed further. However, following Rule 9, the effects of productivity and price changes are reflected in unit costs and hence:

$$\frac{\text{Bus Miles}}{\text{Wages}} \equiv \frac{\text{Bus Miles}}{\text{Men}} \div \frac{\text{Wages}}{\text{Men}}$$

Thus the contribution to output per £ of input cost can be expressed in terms of the input's productivity (bus miles per man) and its unit price (wage costs per man), where the number of men could be replaced by materials volume or capital employed.

In this case study this analysis was only applied to the contribution of staff costs to output. This simplification is justified by the very high proportion (over 75 per cent) of staff cost in total costs. If material costs were thought to be worthy of examination then the practical problem of measuring material volume would have to be overcome. An index number formulation of the type suggested above in respect of output (Chapter 4) could be used, for although such a formulation becomes complex and unwieldy when large numbers of different materials are involved, it often transpires that two or three materials actually determine almost all the variation in the total.

However, in this case it was decided that neither materials at 15 per cent of total costs nor capital at 10 per cent merited further examination. Returning to labour and the determinants of labour's contribution to output (bus miles per £ of wages), ie bus miles per man and wages per man, clearly, following Rule 1, the productivity of labour could be expressed in terms of the productivity of either of the other two factors and the proportion between them and labour eg

$$\frac{\text{Bus Miles}}{\text{Men}} = \frac{\text{Bus Miles}}{\text{Capital Employed}} \times \frac{\text{Capital Employed}}{\text{Men}}$$

where material volume or cost could replace capital employed. In fact, this equation did not prove useful. The measurement of capital employed was regarded as somewhat suspect in the organisation and little substitutability was believed to exist between materials and labour, rendering the proportion between them largely meaningless.

Wages per man can, however, be usefully broken down further to show the impact of changes in hourly wage rates and hours per man ie

$$\frac{\text{Wages}}{\text{Men}} = \frac{\text{Wages}}{\text{Hours}} \times \frac{\text{Hours}}{\text{Men}}$$

This equation gave particularly interesting results in this case as wage rates were negotiated by a central body controlling the organisation while actual hours of work, in particular overtime, were determined locally. The equation thus distinguishes between those elements of wages per man which could be controlled by the organisation at the centre and those which could not.

It may be interesting at this point to note the similarities between the hierarchy illustrated in figure 6.3 and the set of ratios suggested for a batch production engineering firm in Chapter 5, illustrated in figure 5.2. Essentially the ratios which are similar relate to labour productivity and price, viz.

Transport	**Engineering**
bus miles per man	value added per man - labour productivity
average cost per man	wages - price of labour

Apart from these, the dissimilarities arise from the concentration on profit in the engineering case and also the specific difficulties associated with capital measurement in the transport case. Such a difference could well disappear in a private, profit-making transport organisation.

Departmental Approach

A further set of indicators for the organisation as a whole, illustrated in figure 6.4, shows the contribution of the major departments when the initial breakdown of bus miles per £ of cost again follows Rule 3 using the identity:

$$\frac{\text{Bus Miles}}{\text{Cost}} = \frac{\text{Bus Miles}}{\text{Operations Costs}} \times \frac{\text{Operations Costs}}{\text{Cost}}$$

where Operations Costs could be replaced by Engineering Costs, Head Office Costs and Capital Costs, which are not allocated to departments. The proportion of total costs arising in, in this case, the Operations Department can of course be broken down to show the contribution of sub-departments (or cost centres) within departments, as illustrated in Annex 1 to this chapter.

However, a more useful breakdown is probably the one followed in figure 6.4 where the overall contribution to output of each department provides the starting point for an input factor analysis for the department (a la figure 6.3) or an analysis of the contribution of each sub-department and its factor analysis. These analyses are also given in Annex 1 and expanded in the section below on Departmental Performance.

This departmental approach tends to bypass the flowchart analysis of figure 6.1 since it looks at the contribution of all departments to overall performance rather than at their contribution to other departments. However, the heirarchy can easily be modified to show the contribution of, in this case, the Engineering Department to the Operations Department. The modification requires the use of Rule 1, since inputs from other departments can be treated as its own factor inputs by the Operations Department, ie it uses men, materials, capital and the Engineering Department's output. Thus

$$\frac{\text{Garage Output}}{\text{Garage Men}} = \frac{\text{Garage Output}}{\text{Engineering Output}} \times \frac{\text{Engineering Output}}{\text{Garage Men}}$$

Figure 6.5 illustrates the complete heirarchy, which is simply an extended version of part of figure 6.4. The complete set of equations relating to figure 6.5 is given in Annex 1.

Figure 6.4 : Departmental Analysis

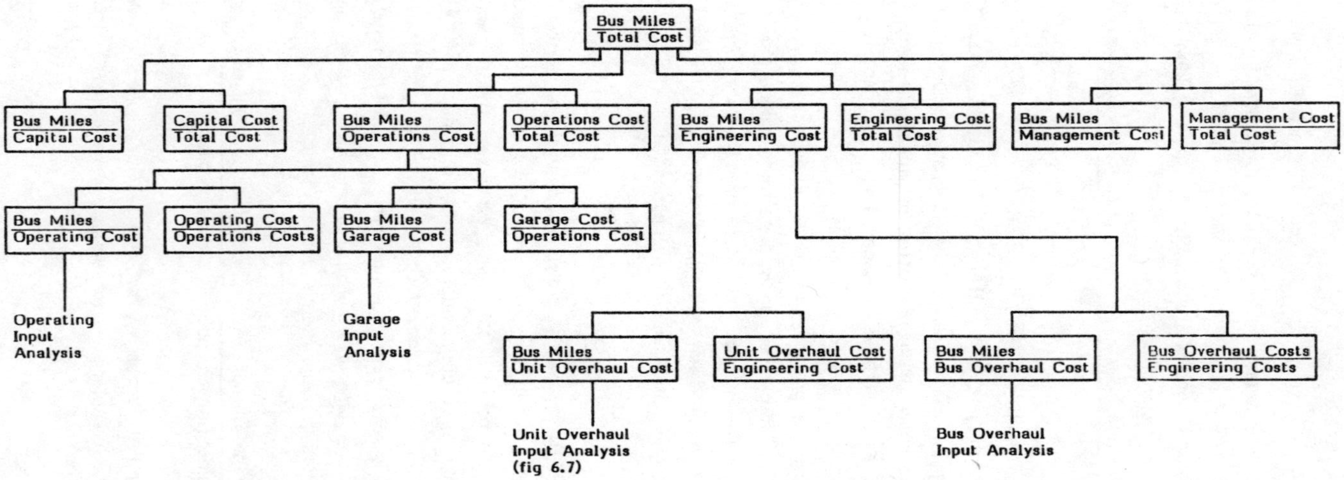

Bus Miles / Total Cost

Bus Miles / Capital Cost
Capital Cost / Total Cost
Bus Miles / Operations Cost
Operations Cost / Total Cost
Bus Miles / Engineering Cost
Engineering Cost / Total Cost
Bus Miles / Management Cost
Management Cost / Total Cost

Bus Miles / Operating Cost
Operating Cost / Operations Costs
Bus Miles / Garage Cost
Garage Cost / Operations Cost

Operating Input Analysis
Garage Input Analysis

Bus Miles / Unit Overhaul Cost
Unit Overhaul Cost / Engineering Cost
Bus Miles / Bus Overhaul Cost
Bus Overhaul Costs / Engineering Costs

Unit Overhaul Input Analysis (fig 6.7)
Bus Overhaul Input Analysis

Figure 6.5 : Sub-Departmental Analysis

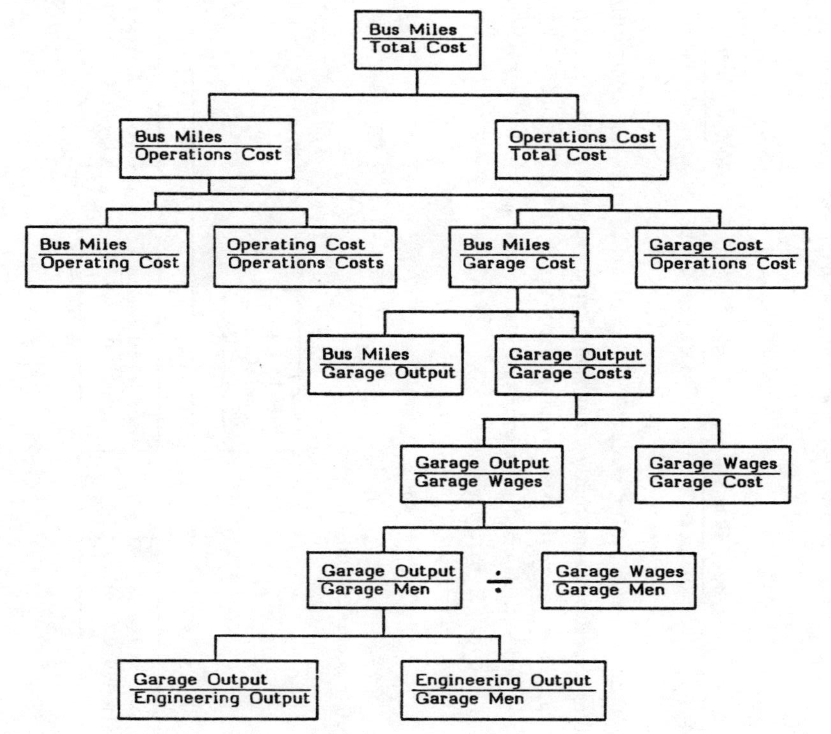

Budget Approach

The final hierarchy for the business as a whole, illustrated in figure 6.6, analyses it in terms of the annual budget. Three factors contribute to internal efficiency: achievement of the output budget (bus miles as a proportion of budgeted miles); achievement of the cost budget (total costs as a proportion of budgeted costs); planned internal efficiency (budgeted miles per £ of budgeted costs), viz:

$$\frac{\text{Bus Miles}}{\text{Cost}} = \frac{\text{Bus Miles}}{\text{Budgeted Miles}} \div \frac{\text{Cost}}{\text{Budgeted Cost}} \times \frac{\text{Bugeted Miles}}{\text{Budgeted Cost}}$$

Obviously each of these ratios could be broken down to show the contribution of particular departments or factors, depending on the detail within the budget. In this case the analysis was used to indicate simply how much actual efficiency varied with planned efficiency and the extent to which the deviation was due to physical or cost deviations.

Figure 6.6 : Budget Analysis

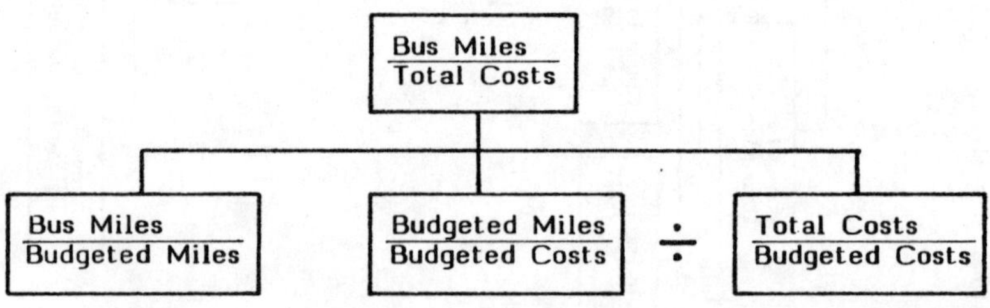

Performance Indicators : Departmental Performance

Figure 6.3 showed how the contribution of each department or sub-department to internal performance could be analysed. Having carried out that analysis, or indeed at the outset of the performance measurement exercise, it may be necessary to measure the performance of the individual department as opposed to the organisation as a whole. As stated above this can be done on the lines of figure 6.2, ie by analysing the contribution of each input factor, and figure 6.7 illustrates the hierarchy for the Unit Overhaul Sub-Department within the Engineering Department in this particular organisation.

Figure 6.7 links into figure 6.4 via the contribution of the whole Engineering Department using the equation

$$\frac{\text{Bus Miles}}{\text{Engineering Cost}} = \frac{\text{Bus Miles}}{\text{Unit Overhaul Cost}} \times \frac{\text{Unit Overhaul Cost}}{\text{Engineering Cost}}$$

The output of the Unit Overhaul Department itself is then measured as described earlier in this chapter and the rest of the hierarchy is on the same lines as figure 6.3, with two specific differences.

First, following Rule 3, since materials constitute nearly as large a cost share as labour in this particular department, they are analysed in rather more detail, using Rule 2 and the equation

$$\frac{\text{Unit Overhaul Output}}{\text{Material Cost}} = \frac{\text{Unit Overhaul Output}}{\text{Material Volume}} \div \frac{\text{Material Cost}}{\text{Material Volume}}$$

where material cost per unit of materials is average material price. Although a very large number of materials are used in the works a relatively small number account for a high proportion of the total material cost and an index number formulation as described above (Chapter 4) could be used to measure material (volume).

Second, the analysis of labour's contribution, particularly its physical contribution, is more detailed than for the organisation as a whole and incorporates performance measures that were already in use in the works. The works operated an incentive scheme which used 'standard hours' for staff within the scheme. Thus labour productivity (unit overhaul output per man) is broken down to show how this measure (standard hours per work measured man) relates to the hierarchy, ie

Figure 6.7 : Departmental Input Analysis : Unit Overhauls

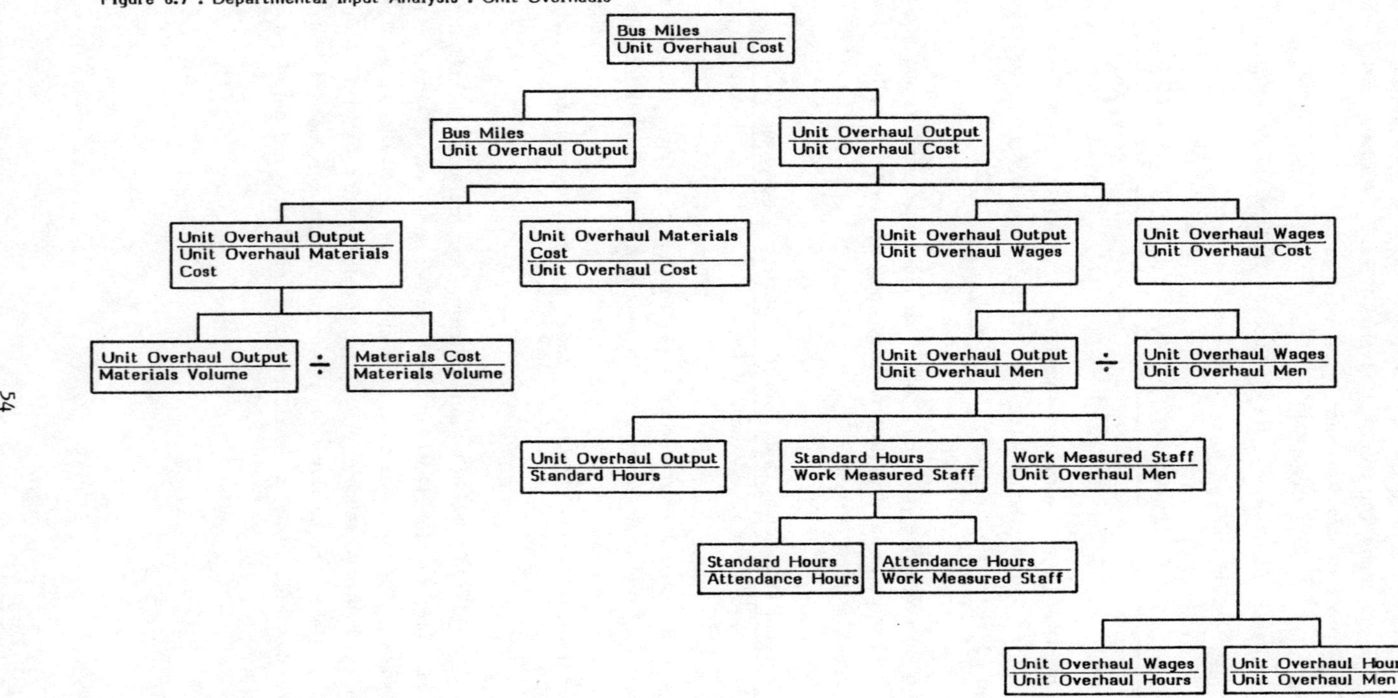

$$\frac{\text{Unit Overhaul Output}}{\text{Men}} = \frac{\text{Unit Overhaul Output}}{\text{Standard Hours}} \times \frac{\text{Standard Hours}}{\text{Work Measured Men}} \times \frac{\text{Work Measured Men}}{\text{Men}}$$

In the short term, the proportion of work measured staff in the total tends not to change and so the variation in labour productivity can be explained in terms of the exisiting incentive scheme measure of productivity (standard hours per work measured man) and the rate at which standard hours are translated into output (unit overhaul output per standard hour).

The inclusion of this equation proved to be particularly important in this case since past improvements in standard hours per work measured man had led to the conclusion that labour productivity was improving. In fact, the level of output per standard hour had actually been falling and had led to a **fall** in labour productivity, measured by output per man. Such a situation highlights the dangers inherent in using isolated measures of performance and not relating them to the overall structure.

Figure 6.7 shows that standard hours per work measured man can be broken down to look at hourly productivity (standard hours per attendance hour) and attendance rates. Such measures are obviously in common use in many manufacturing concerns, particularly those with hourly paid staff.

Conclusions

This case study highlighted the importance of a number of the steps and rules set out in Chapter 3. In particular, a great deal of time was spent following Step 1 and clarifying the exact nature of the business or departments and their outputs. Thereafter Rules 2 and 3 proved particularly useful in deciding how to incoporate all the relevant factors.

However, three additional rules emerged which are of particular relevance in divisionalised or departmentalised organisations.

Rule 5

In an organisation with more than one department the output of each department must be related to the output of the organisation as a whole (eg from figure 6.7, Bus miles per unit of Unit Overhaul Output). This keeps in perspective the relative importance of each department and the utilisation of its output.

Rule 6

Ratios concerning input factor performance which appear in the hierarchy for the organisation as a whole (ie figure 6.3) must also appear in the hierarchy for each department (see figure 6.7). The former are merely weighted sums of the latter. The reverse, of course, is not necessarily true. Many ratios may be of importance at departmental level which are of no interest at the level of the organisation as a whole (eg material cost per unit of material, standard hours per attendance hour).

Rule 7

The overall objective of each department must be expressed in terms of the objective of the organisation as a whole, eg that of the Unit Overhaul Department in this case is Bus Miles per £ of Unit Overhaul cost. This is not to say that its **performance** will be measured in those terms since its output may not be the same as that of the overall organisation. For instance, in this case the organisation's objective is to maximise Bus Miles per £ of cost. The Unit Overhaul Department's objective must be to maximise Bus Miles per £ of Unit Overhaul Cost. If it seeks only to maximise its own performance (Unit Overhaul Output per £ of Unit Overhaul Cost) it may produce wasteful output, given the level of Bus Miles, and hence reduce Bus Miles per Unit of Unit Overhaul Output, have no useful effect on Bus Miles per £ of Unit Overhaul Cost and hence Bus Miles per £ of total cost.

In Annex 2 to this chapter some sample results have been put on part of the hierarchy discussed in the chapter to illustrate how it was used to analyse the past performance of the works.

Annex 1 to Chapter 6 : The Departmental Approach Extended

1) Analyses of Departmental Cost Proportions

$$\frac{\text{Operations Cost}}{\text{Cost}} = \frac{\text{Operating Cost}}{\text{Cost}} \div \frac{\text{Operating Cost}}{\text{Operations Cost}}$$

$$\frac{\text{Operations Cost}}{\text{Cost}} = \frac{\text{Garage Cost}}{\text{Cost}} \div \frac{\text{Garage Cost}}{\text{Operations Cost}}$$

2) Analyses of Departments and/or sub-departments by inputs

$$\frac{\text{Bus Miles}}{\text{Operations Cost}} = \frac{\text{Bus Miles}}{\text{Operating Cost}} \times \frac{\text{Operating Costs}}{\text{Operations Cost}}$$

$$\frac{\text{Bus Miles}}{\text{Operations Cost}} = \frac{\text{Bus Miles}}{\text{Garage Costs}} \times \frac{\text{Garage Costs}}{\text{Operations Costs}}$$

$$\frac{\text{Bus Miles}}{\text{Operating Costs}} = \frac{\text{Bus Miles}}{\text{Operating Output}} \times \frac{\text{Operating Output}}{\text{Operating Costs}}$$

where Operating Department output could be replaced by Garage Department output. The rest of the hierarchy would be a breakdown of Operating Output per £ of Operating Costs or Garage Output per £ of Garage Costs as in figure 6.3 or as appropriate by department.

3) Complete Analyses of Bus Miles per £ of Cost by Department and Departmental Input Factors

$$\frac{\text{Bus Miles}}{\text{Cost}} = \frac{\text{Bus Miles}}{\text{Operations Cost}} \times \frac{\text{Operations Cost}}{\text{Cost}}$$

$$\frac{\text{Bus Miles}}{\text{Operations Cost}} = \frac{\text{Bus Miles}}{\text{Garage Costs}} \times \frac{\text{Garage Costs}}{\text{Operations Cost}}$$

$$\frac{\text{Bus Miles}}{\text{Garage Costs}} = \frac{\text{Bus Miles}}{\text{Garage Output}} \times \frac{\text{Garage Output}}{\text{Garage Costs}}$$

$$\frac{\text{Garage Output}}{\text{Garage Costs}} = \frac{\text{Garage Output}}{\text{Garage Wages}} \times \frac{\text{Garage Wages}}{\text{Garage Costs}}$$

$$\frac{\text{Garage Output}}{\text{Garage Wages}} = \frac{\text{Garage Output}}{\text{Men}} \div \frac{\text{Garage Wages}}{\text{Men}}$$

$$\frac{\text{Garage Output}}{\text{Men}} = \frac{\text{Garage Output}}{\text{Engineering Output}} \times \frac{\text{Engineering Output}}{\text{(garage) Men}}$$

Annex 2 to Chapter 6 : Sample Results

A6.1 In figure 6.8 sample results are given linking the hierarchies shown in figures 6.4 and 6.7 of the main text, to show how, in this case, changes in labour productivity in one department affect internal efficiency.

A6.2 Figure 6.8 shows that, while attendance per man (1) rose the productivity of each hour (2) fell so standard hours per man (3) rose more slowly. The increase was, however, more than offset by a decline in the amount of output associated with each standard hour (4), and so output per man (5) fell. As wages per man (6) rose at the same time output per £ of wages (7) fell even faster.

A6.3 The impact of this fall on overall sub-departmental performance (8) was determined by the share of wages in total sub-departmental costs (9), and in turn the impact of declining sub-departmental productivity (8) was offset somewhat by improved utilisation of sub-departmental output (10), resulting in a smaller decline in sub-departmental contribution to overall output (11).

A6.4 This decline resulted in a decline in the department's contribution to overall output (12) in proportion to the sub-department's share of departmental costs (13), and that decline, in turn tempered by the department's share of total business costs (14), resulted in a small decline in overall performance (15).

A6.5 In this way the impact of changing attendance hours or the hourly productivity level in one sub-department on the overall performance of the business can be assessed.

A6.6 This method of presenting results is discussed in more detail in Chapter 8. The example does not make use of real data and is for illustrative purposes only.

Annex 2 to Chapter 6, Figure 6.8 : Sample Results for (parts of) Figs. 6.4 and 6.7 to show the impact of changes in labour productivity in one sub-department on overall performance.

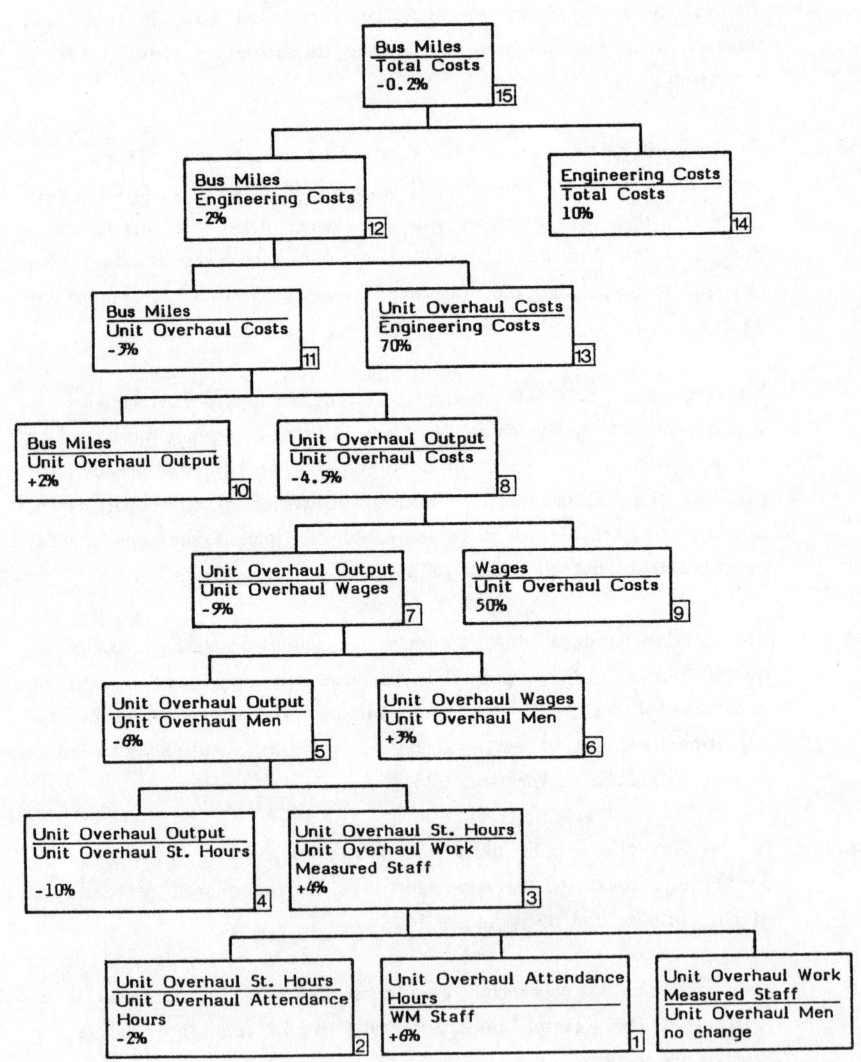

7 Sales and Distribution — Case Study III

This final case study involves the application of the ratio hierarchy method of performance measurement in an organisation concerned with selling and distribution. Some elements of the hierarchy developed relate to the sale and distribution of the particular product concerned and those will not be presented here. The chapter will concentrate rather on those aspects of the case study which are generalisable to other organisations involved in similar activities. The project was undertaken in order to improve the corporate planning facilities of the organisation and the results are now in regular use.

Distinguishing Features of the Organisation

The organisation is in fact part of a larger concern responsible for manufacturing, selling and distributing the product concerned. It thus faces a sole supplier and, in effect, fixed input prices. The distribution system involves significant quantities of capital equipment. The product is not perishable and no storage costs are involved.

The management wished to reflect two parallel structures in the measurement hierarchy; the departmental structure (finance, engineering and commercial) and the account heading (or activity) structure (distribution, customer service, accounts, administration, training and welfare). They also wished to consider specifically the performance of the physical distribution system and the impact of customer profile and payment methods. Finally, since goods are invoiced after delivery, they were particularly concerned about cash flow and the level of bad debts.

In contrast to the previous case study the measurement of both the objective of the organistion and its output were relatively straightforward. The objective was generally accepted to be defined as return on capital while a physical measure of output volume was readily available. Since the output is sold in a free market the total sales or revenue figure is also available and meaningful, but given the organisation's lack of control over the price of its major input, the 'bought out' element, added value is clearly a more relevant measure.

Performance Indicators: Overall Performance

It is fortunate that such measures are available since the very extensive requirements of the measurement system from management necessitate a fairly complex model. Reference to figure 7.1 may help the reader follow the analysis.

Given the importance of value added the initial breakdown of return on capital is the fairly obvious one already used in the engineering case study, ie

$$\frac{\text{Profit}}{\text{Capital Employed}} = \frac{\text{Profit}}{\text{Value Added}} \times \frac{\text{Value Added}}{\text{Capital Employed}}$$

The share of profit in value added can then be broken down to show the contribution of the marketing side of the business, using the breakdown

$$\frac{\text{Profit}}{\text{Value Added}} = \frac{\text{Profit}}{\text{Customer}} \div \frac{\text{Value Added}}{\text{Customer}}$$

It can also be broken down to show the contribution of the physical distribution system using

$$\frac{\text{Profit}}{\text{Value Added}} = \frac{\text{Profit}}{\text{Bought Out Items}} \times \frac{\text{Bought Out Items}}{\text{Value Added}}$$

The other side of the original breakdown of return on capital (Value Added/Capital Employed) can then be broken down to show the specific contributions of the labour force and the capital invested in the business since

$$\frac{\text{Value Added}}{\text{Capital Employed}} = \frac{\text{Value Added}}{\text{Output}} \times \frac{\text{Output}}{\text{Capital Employed}}$$

Value Added/Output leads directly into a breakdown by cost categories ie

Figure 7.1 : Overall Ratio Hierarchy Structure

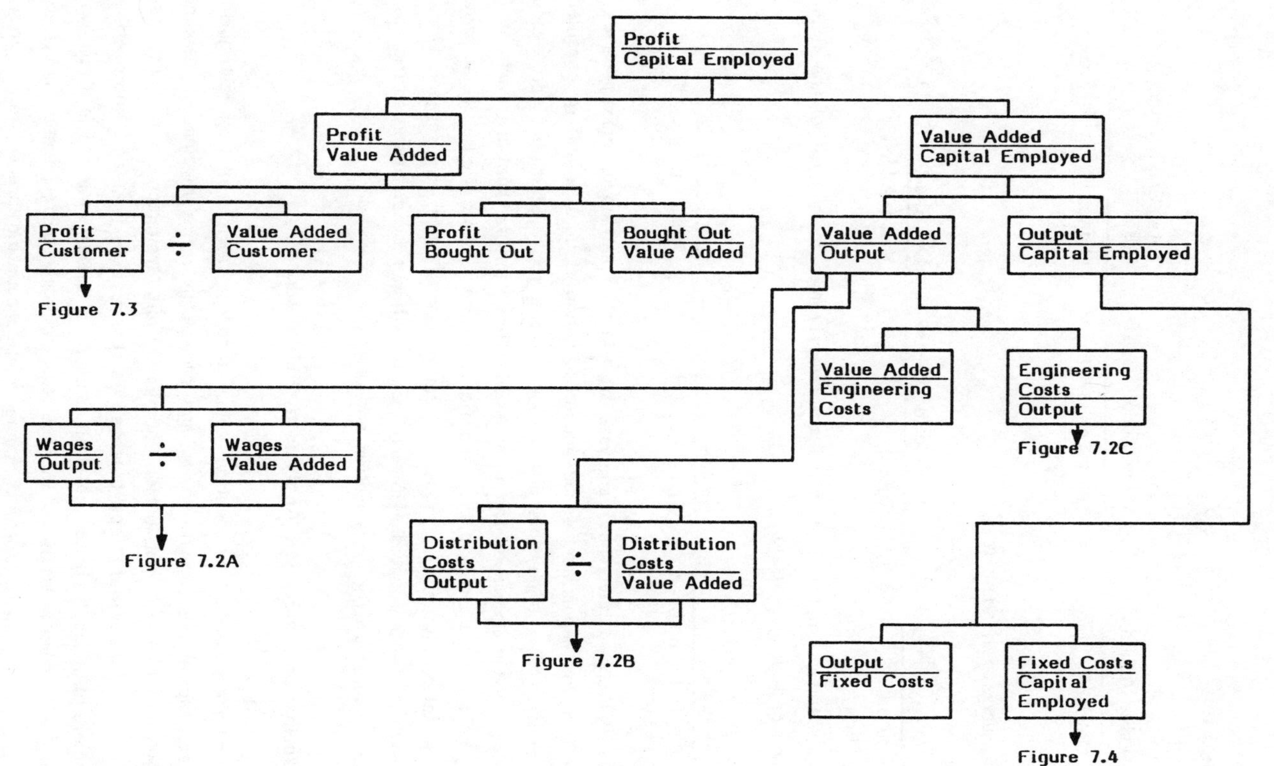

$$\frac{\text{Value Added}}{\text{Output}} = \frac{\text{Wages}}{\text{Output}} \div \frac{\text{Wages}}{\text{Value Added}}$$

by department ie

$$\frac{\text{Value Added}}{\text{Output}} = \frac{\text{Value Added}}{\text{Total Engineering Costs}} \times \frac{\text{Total Engineering Costs}}{\text{Output}}$$

and by account heading ie

$$\frac{\text{Value Added}}{\text{Output}} = \frac{\text{Distribution Costs}}{\text{Output}} \div \frac{\text{Distribution Costs}}{\text{Value Added}}$$

Output/Capital Employed in turn leads directly into an analysis of the fixed and working capital split using

$$\frac{\text{Output}}{\text{Capital Employed}} = \frac{\text{Output}}{\text{Fixed Capital}} \times \frac{\text{Fixed Capital}}{\text{Capital Employed}}$$

Figure 7.1 shows how these analyses fit together and cover management's wish to reflect the departmental and account heading structures and to consider the performance of the physical distribution system, the marketing function and the working capital assets of the business. In the following sections each of these analyses are considered in turn and figures 7.2-4 fit into figure 7.1 as shown to give a totally integrated model of the performance of the organisation. The analysis of the physical distribution system will not be discussed further as it is totally specific to the organisation and product concerned.

Performance Indicators: Analysis of Value Added

The company wished to analyse value added in terms of cost categories (ie wages, capital costs, other costs and profit); in terms of account headings or 'activities', such as distribution, administration, training and welfare; and in terms of functional departments, in this case finance, engineering and commercial. Clearly it is this last, and to a lesser extent the first, analysis which will enable them to manage the company better; analysis by account heading fits in with current management accounting practice but since the account headings do not correspond to lines of authority or responsibility it provides information which is interesting rather than useful.

Figure 7.2A shows a breakdown of Value Added/Output to show the contribution of labour costs and any other cost element of Value Added in which there might be interest. The analysis of labour costs will be familiar in that it makes use of Rule 2, ie

$$\frac{\text{Wages}}{\text{Output}} = \frac{\text{Wages}}{\text{Men}} \div \frac{\text{Output}}{\text{Men}}$$

and Rule 1, ie

$$\frac{\text{Output}}{\text{Men}} = \frac{\text{Output}}{\text{Capital Employed}} \times \frac{\text{Capital Employed}}{\text{Men}}$$

In addition, Wages per man can of course be broken down to show an hourly analysis, ie

$$\frac{\text{Wages}}{\text{Men}} = \frac{\text{Wages}}{\text{Attendance Hours}} \times \frac{\text{Attendance Hours}}{\text{Men}}$$

as in the transport case study. This, of course, provides a very general analysis of labour's performance which would be of interest to top management only. More specific measures are included in the departmental analysis.

Non-labour elements of value added can be analysed as shown in figure 7.2A, where rates have been taken as a particular example, ie

$$\frac{\text{Wages}}{\text{Value Added}} = \frac{\text{Wages}}{\text{Other Costs}} \times \frac{\text{Other Costs}}{\text{Value Added}}$$

$$\frac{\text{Other Costs}}{\text{Value Added}} = \frac{\text{Rates}}{\text{Value Added}} \div \frac{\text{Rates}}{\text{Other Costs}}$$

The share of rates, for instance, in non-staff costs can then be analysed further if it appears to be significant.

The organisation had a management accounting system whlch identified five activities: distribution, accounting (ie billing and receiving payments), customer

Figure 7.2A : Breakdown by Input Cost Categories

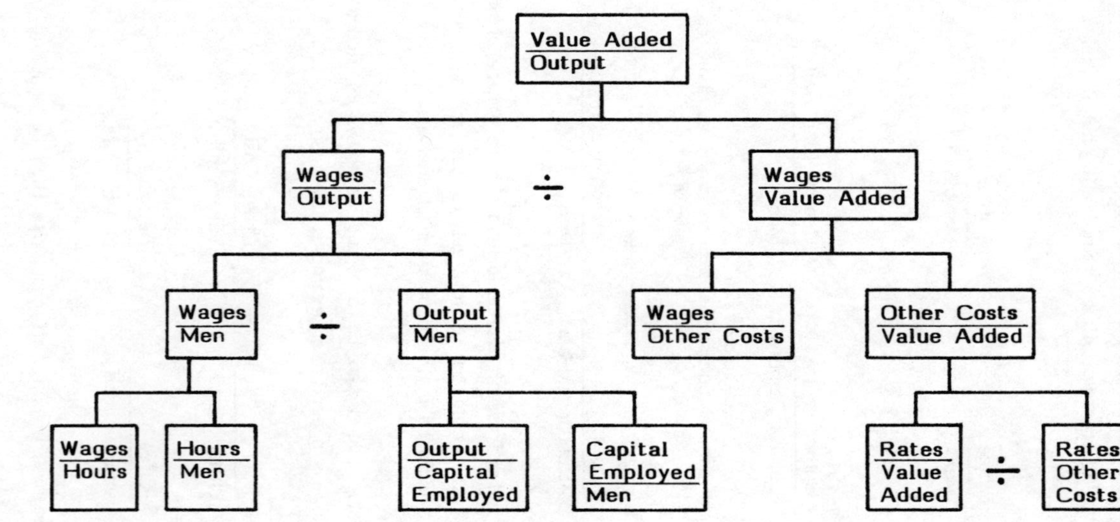

service, administration, and training and welfare. In the case of each activity, management was interested in its cost per unit of output and its share of total value added; its cost per customer; its salary cost per customer and its salary cost as a proportion of its total cost. In addition, training and welfare costs, and training costs separately, had to be related to numbers employed.

The result is shown in figure 7.2B and is presented for illustrative purposes only; little managerial action could be based on such information since the activities cut across several lines of responsibility. The company was unwise in attempting to base a performance measurement model on account headings simply because they are in current use but good could come of the exercise; the uselessness of the resultant information could result in a change in the management accounting system.

Figure 7.2C, however, illustrates a much more useful analysis in which the contributions of specific functions within departments and of particular types of labour are analysed. The (slightly adapted) example taken is of the engineering department. It has three major functions: to maintain the distribution system; to service existing customers; to set up service to new customers. Hence the initial breakdown of Value Added/Output using

$$\frac{\text{Value Added}}{\text{Output}} = \frac{\text{Value Added}}{\text{Engineering Cost}} \times \frac{\text{Engineering Cost}}{\text{Output}}$$

$$\frac{\text{Engineering Cost}}{\text{Output}} = \frac{\text{System Maintenance Cost}}{\text{Output}} \div \frac{\text{System Maintenance Cost}}{\text{Engineering Costs}}$$

This analysis is essentially similar to that used in the transport case study.

Maintenance costs per unit of output can in this case be broken down to show the cost per element of the system, ie

$$\frac{\text{System Maintenance Costs}}{\text{Output}} = \frac{\text{System Maintenance Costs}}{\text{Machines}} \div \frac{\text{Output}}{\text{Machines}}$$

where 'machine' is an element of the system which has been maintained. System Maintenance Costs per machine can then be analysed to show the contribution of labour and other costs, ie

Figure 7.2B : Breakdown by Account Heading

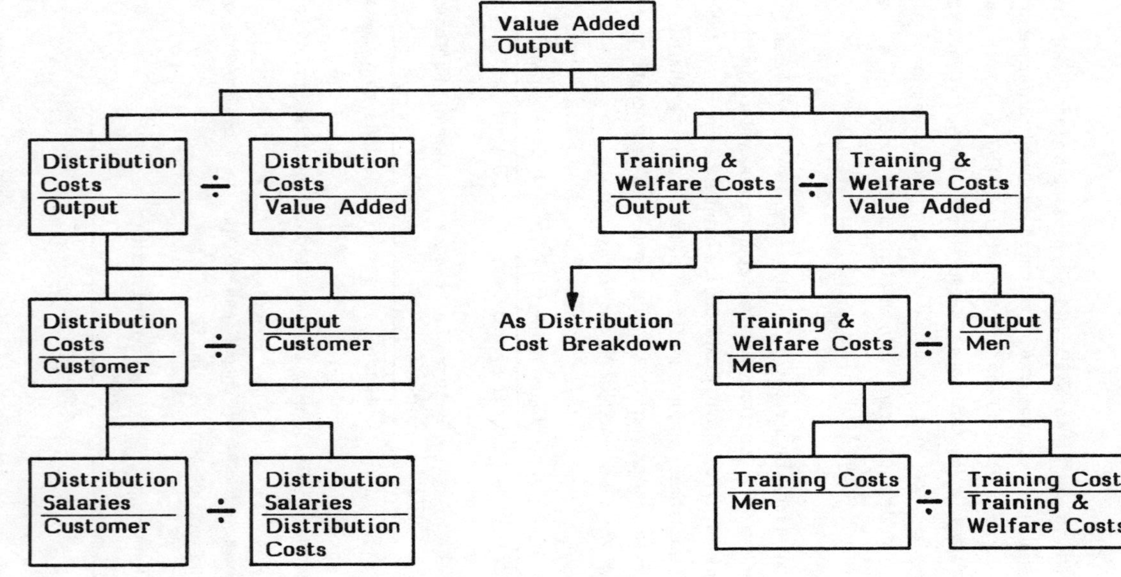

NB: Distribution Costs could be replaced by Customer Service, Accounts or Administrative Costs.

Figure 7.2C : Analysis by Department

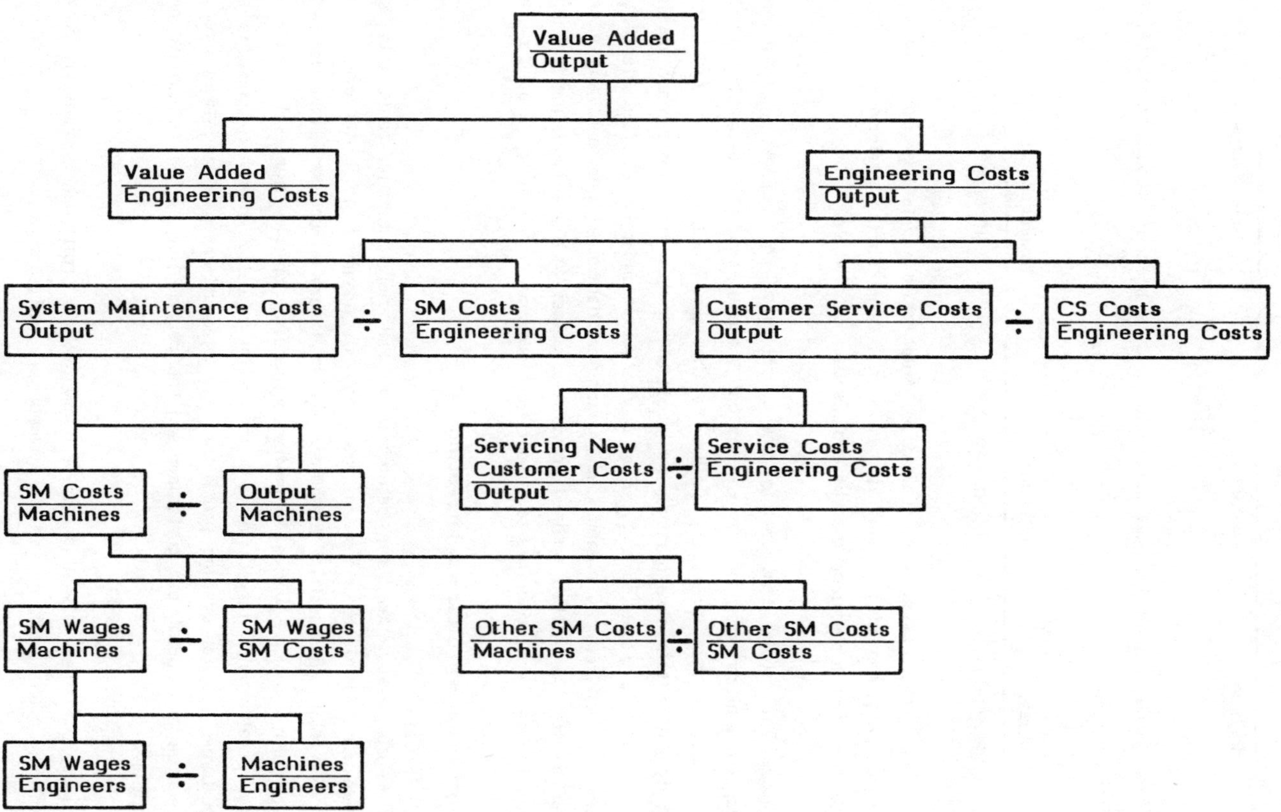

$$\frac{\text{System Maintenance Costs}}{\text{Machines}} = \frac{\text{System Maintenance Wages}}{\text{Machines}} \div \frac{\text{System Maintenance Wages}}{\text{System Maintenance Costs}}$$

These costs can in turn be analysed to give specific labour productivity measures, eg

$$\frac{\text{System Maintenance Wages}}{\text{Machine}} = \frac{\text{System Maintenance Wages}}{\text{Engineer}} \div \frac{\text{Machines}}{\text{Engineer}}$$

The number of machines maintained per engineer is a very specific measure of productivity and in this way it has been related to the performance of the function, the department and the organisation as a whole.

Figure 7.2C shows that each of the functions of the engineering department can be analysed in a similar way, as can those of the other departments. This approach is thus essentially similar to that developed in the transport case study but in this case management requested greater detail and more specific measures where particular types of labour were concerned. At first glance the link between return on capital and machines maintained per man may appear remote but the method outlined provides a logical way of establishing that link, which must be done before such specific measures can be of any practical use.

Performance Indicators: Marketing

The organisation has three categories of customer, domestic, commercial and industrial. Domestic customers can pay in advance or in arrears while commercial and industrial customers pay in arrears either monthly or quarterly. The price charged varies somewhat according to the type of customer. Essentially an analysis of the marketing situation needs to consider the customer profile; average prices per customer category, arising from average revenue and output per customer; and the contribution of the various payment options.

Figure 7.3 shows how this can be done. Initially profit per customer is broken down into the profit margin and revenue per customer, ie

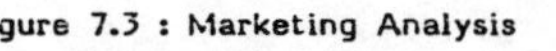

Figure 7.3 : Marketing Analysis

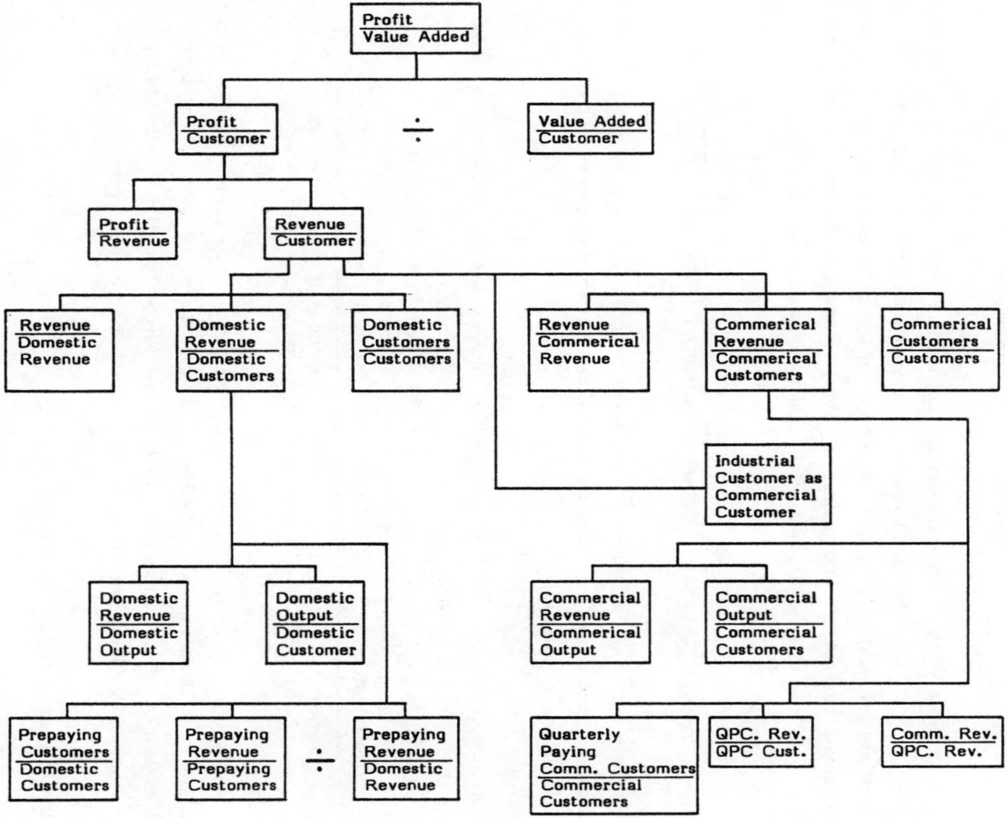

$$\frac{\text{Profit}}{\text{Customer}} = \frac{\text{Profit}}{\text{Revenue}} \times \frac{\text{Revenue}}{\text{Customer}}$$

This latter then forms the basis for an analysis by customer type ie

$$\frac{\text{Revenue}}{\text{Customer}} = \frac{\text{Revenue}}{\text{Domestic Revenue}} \times \frac{\text{Domestic Revenue}}{\text{Domestic Customer}} \times \frac{\text{Domestic Customer}}{\text{Customer}}$$

and similarly for other customer categories. Revenue per £ of domestic revenue and domestic customers as a proportion of total customers are both measures of customer profile, in terms of revenue share and number share. Domestic revenue per domestic customer, however, reflects average customer size in terms of revenue, and price, and can be analysed accordingly, ie

$$\frac{\text{Domestic Revenue}}{\text{Domestic Customer}} = \frac{\text{Domestic Revenue}}{\text{Domestic Output}} \times \frac{\text{Domestic Output}}{\text{Domestic Customer}}$$

Domestic revenue per unit of domestic output is average price paid by domestic customers and domestic output per domestic customer is their average size in volume terms.

Revenue per customer type can also be broken down to show the contribution of the payment method, eg

$$\frac{\text{Domestic Revenue}}{\text{Domestic Customer}} = \frac{\text{Prepaying Customers}}{\text{Domestic Customers}} \times \frac{\text{Prepaid Revenue}}{\text{Prepaying Customer}} \div \frac{\text{Prepaid Revenue}}{\text{Domestic Revenue}}$$

This type of analysis could be easily adapted to customer profiles in other sectors of industry and provides a clear and logical way of assessing the contribution of each customer type to overall profitability, hence assisting the marketing decision concerning areas of greater or lesser concentration.

Performance Indicators: Capital

Finally the management of the organisation was concerned to measure the performance of its working capital, its liquidity and, in particular, its bad debt situation. Such an analysis could clearly be relevant in any business and the hierarchy presented in figure 7.4 is no more than a suggestion as to how it might be done. Many of the ratios involved will be very familiar and in regular use; the point of including them is to show how they too can form part of an integrated performance measurement system.

Figure 7.4 shows that the share of fixed capital in capital employed can be broken down into the relationships between fixed and working capital, and working capital and revenue, and capital turn, ie

$$\frac{\text{Fixed Capital}}{\text{Capital Employed}} = \frac{\text{Fixed Capital}}{\text{Working Capital}} \times \frac{\text{Working Capital}}{\text{Revenue}} \times \frac{\text{Revenue}}{\text{Capital Employed}}$$

The relationship between fixed and working capital can then be analysed further to look at the liquidity situation, ie

$$\frac{\text{Fixed Capital}}{\text{Working Capital}} = \frac{\text{Fixed Capital}}{\text{Output}} \times \frac{\text{Output}}{\text{Working Capital}}$$

and

$$\frac{\text{Output}}{\text{Working Capital}} = \frac{\text{Output}}{\text{Current Assets}} \times \frac{\text{Current Assets}}{\text{Current Liabilities}} \times \frac{\text{Current Liabilities}}{\text{Working Capital}}$$

Current assets/current liabilities is the commonly used liquidity ratio. Meanwhile working capital in relation to revenue can be broken down to show the impact of debtors in general and bad debts in particular, since

$$\frac{\text{Working Capital}}{\text{Revenue}} = \frac{\text{Debtors}}{\text{Revenue}} \div \frac{\text{Debtors}}{\text{Working Capital}}$$

and

$$\frac{\text{Debtors}}{\text{Revenue}} = \frac{\text{Bad Debtors}}{\text{Revenue}} \div \frac{\text{Bad Debtors}}{\text{Debtors}}$$

Obviously the level of bad debts can also be related to the number of

Figure 7.4 : Working Capital Analysis

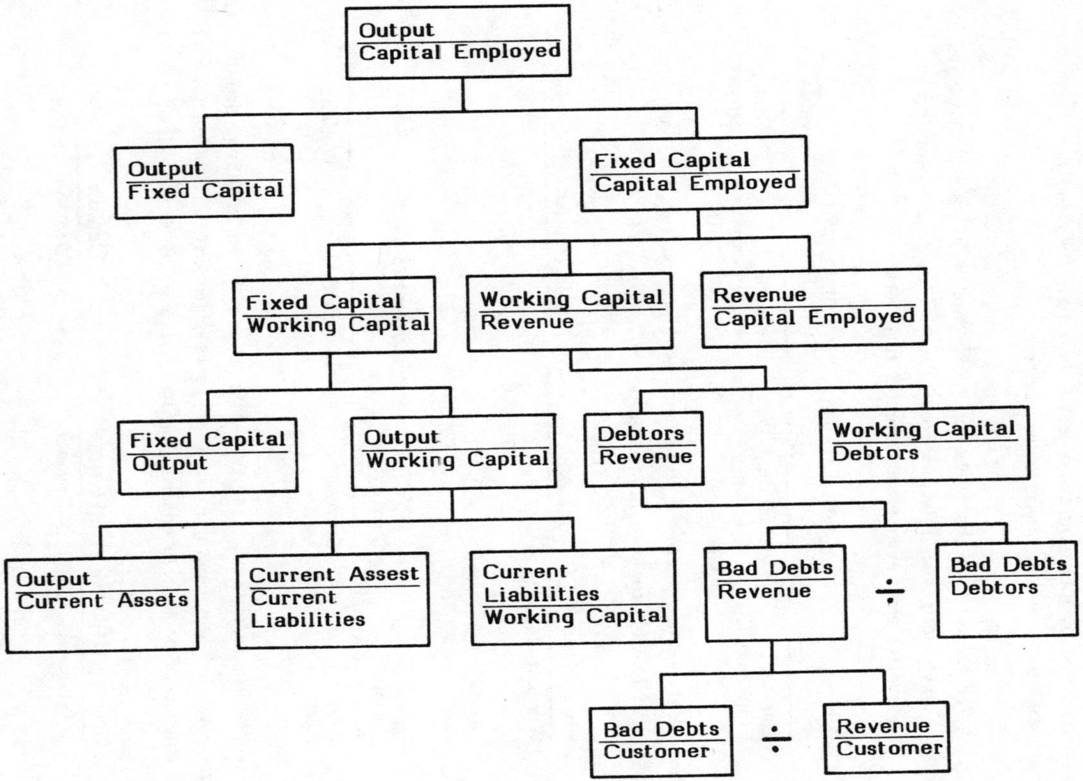

Output / Capital Employed

Output / Fixed Capital

Fixed Capital / Capital Employed

Fixed Capital / Working Capital

Working Capital / Revenue

Revenue / Capital Employed

Fixed Capital / Output

Output / Working Capital

Debtors / Revenue

Working Capital / Debtors

Output / Current Assets

Current Assest / Current Liabilities

Current Liabilities / Working Capital

Bad Debts / Revenue ÷ Bad Debts / Debtors

Bad Debts / Customer ÷ Revenue / Customer

customers via

$$\frac{\text{Bad Debts}}{\text{Revenue}} = \frac{\text{Bad Debts}}{\text{Customer}} \div \frac{\text{Revenue}}{\text{Customer}}$$

Conclusions

Clearly this case study has followed some of the lines of the engineering study - particularly in terms of the overall measures used - and some of the lines of the transport study - in its analysis of labour and departmental performance. It has, however, introduced new analyses by looking specifically at the market profile and the capital structure of the organisation.

It is hoped that these analyses will be of general use outside the distribution sector but in many ways the most useful lesson to be learnt from this case study is a more fundamental one. Any part of a business is susceptible to ratio analysis and the hierarchy of ratios management thinks it wants can always be produced. It is in sorting out which ratios are really useful and actually assist management to manage that the skill and the power of the technique lie.

8 The Presentation of Performance Analysis Results

The last three chapters have described how the job of measuring performance has been tackled in three different sectors of industry. No measurement system will be any use, however, unless the results it produces are presented in such a way that they can be readily understood and facilitate discussion of the performance of the business. In this chapter, one method of achieving such a presentation is described.

For the purposes of illustration this chapter makes use of the set of ratios suggested in the Passenger Transport case study described in Chapter 6, illustrated in figure 6.3 (repeated here for ease of reference) and expressed as the following set of equations:

$$\frac{\text{Bus Miles}}{\text{Cost}} = \frac{\text{Bus Miles}}{\text{Wages}} \times \frac{\text{Wages}}{\text{Cost}}$$

$$\frac{\text{Bus Miles}}{\text{Wages}} = \frac{\text{Bus Miles}}{\text{Men}} \div \frac{\text{Wages}}{\text{Men}}$$

$$\frac{\text{Wages}}{\text{Men}} = \frac{\text{Wages}}{\text{Paid Hours}} \times \frac{\text{Paid Hours}}{\text{Men}}$$

The data in the example are not real data. Values have been set against each variable involved in the hierarchy so that results can be calculated and their presentation illustrated. A six-year historical period has been chosen and the forecasts for a budget year have also been included. Annual observations may not always be the most appropriate for monitoring purposes as a shorter time span may be needed, but they would almost certainly be essential for planning purposes (see discussion on the frequency of data in Chapter 9). In any case, the same logic concerning presentation can be applied over any period and number of observations.

The base data, ratio calculations and rates of change are shown in figure 8.1:

Figure 8.1 **Sample Bus Data 1977-1983**

(All financial data expressed in £'000 at 1982 prices)

	1977	1978	1979	1980	1981	1982	1983*
Bus Miles	180	170	165	175	175	165	170
Costs	395	400	420	415	415	405	410
Wages	275	285	285	290	305	300	305
Men	315	315	310	305	310	300	300
Paid Hours	75	70	70	65	70	65	70
Bus Miles/Cost	0.46	0.43	0.39	0.42	0.42	0.41	0.41
Bus Miles/Wages	0.65	0.60	0.58	0.60	0.57	0.55	0.56
Wages/Cost	69.6%	71.3%	67.9%	69.9%	73.5%	74.1%	74.4%
Bus Miles/Men	0.57	0.54	0.53	0.57	0.56	0.55	0.57
Wages/Men	0.87	0.90	0.92	0.95	0.98	1.00	1.02
Wages/Paid Hours	3.67	4.07	4.07	4.46	4.36	4.62	4.36
Paid Hours/Men	0.24	0.22	0.23	0.21	0.23	0.22	0.23

Percentage Changes

	1982/1977	1982/1981	1983*/1982
Bus Miles/Costs	-10.9	- 2.4	No change
Bus Miles/Wages	-15.4	- 3.5	+1.8
Bus Miles/Men	- 3.5	- 1.8	+3.6
Wages/Men	+14.9	+ 2.0	+2.0
Wages/Paid Hours	+25.9	+ 6.0	-5.6
Paid Hours/Men	- 8.3	- 4.3	+4.5

* forecast

All financial data must be expressed in real terms, ie the inflationary element must be removed. How this can be done is discussed in the next chapter but whichever method is used there is much to be said for expressing the series in the prices of the most recent year (in this case, 1982) as these are the prices which are most readily understood.

The presentational problem is that figure 8.1 is difficult to interpret. The linkage between the ratios is not clear. The trend over time is confusing because so much information is being presented in one table. A method of presentation is therefore required which will:

a) clarify and draw attention to the links between the ratios and hence to any underlying causal relationships;

b) be readily assimilated; and

c) display recent changes, trends in ratios and absolute values where appropriate.

A method which accomplishes these three objectives is illustrated in figure 8.2. Each ratio is incorporated in a box, the contents of which are:

(i) the name of the ratio
(ii) its definition
(iii) the change in its value over the whole period
(iv) the change in its value over the most recent period
(v) the change in its value over the forecast period
(vi) its graph number

eg
i) INTERNAL EFFICIENCY
ii) BUS MILES/TOTAL COSTS
iii) 6-YEAR CHANGE (%)
iv) 1-YEAR CHANGE (%)
v) BUDGET YEAR CHANGE (%)
vi) 1

Elements iii), iv) and v) may be altered depending on the time span considered. Where it is not the percentage change over time which is of interest but the absolute value of the ratio, they may be replaced by an average or one or more particular values. In this example this applies to the third ratio, wages as a proportion of total costs, in figure 8.2.

Figure 8.2 : Presentation of Results in Figure 8.1

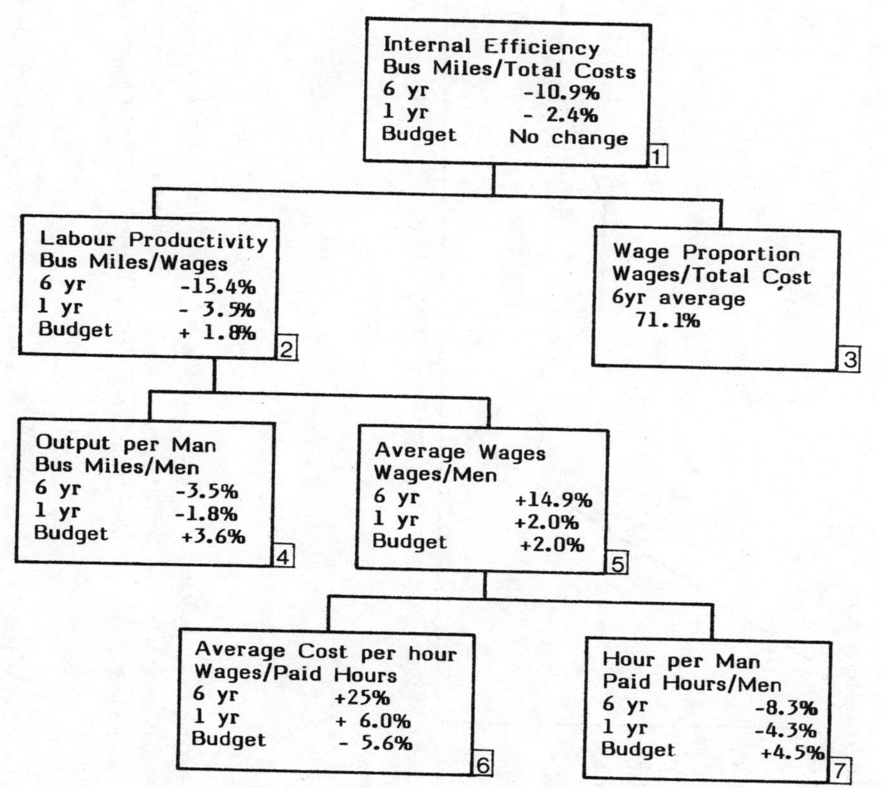

For maximum effect the boxes should all be presented on one piece of paper. Where the hierarchy is too extensive to allow this, the ratio linking one page with another should be repeated to ensure that the linkage is clear. It is also suggested that the result hierarchy be accompanied by a set of graphs, one for each ratio, so that any ratio can be studied in greater detail if necessary and, in particular, the events in the years not subject to numerical analysis in the boxes can be studied. Figures 8.3 and 8.6 show such graphs.

Figure 8.3 : Sample Graph of Internal Efficiency

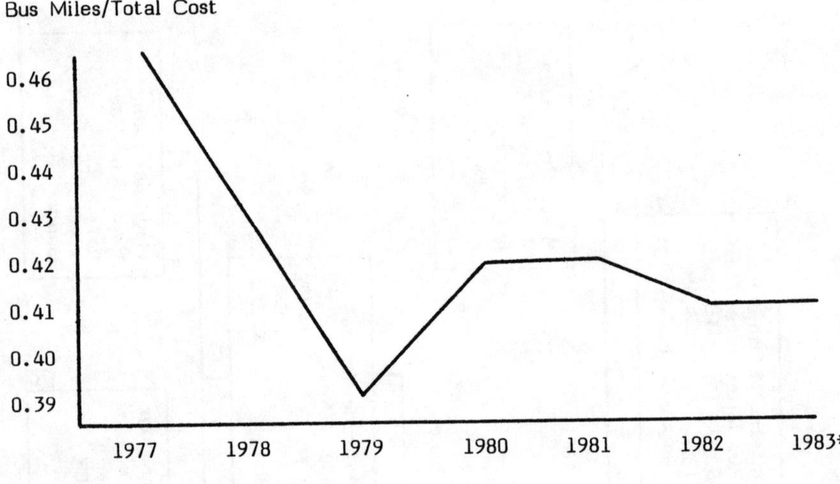

*forecast

A document incorporating results in the form of figure 8.2 and supporting graphs presents the results of a ratio analysis exercise in a clear and comprehensive fashion which aids constructive debate and fruitful use of the ratios.

When the object of the performance measurement exercise is to compare two or more like businesses, either there will be a figure 8.2 for each business or one diagram can show the most recent change for each of them. If only one period's data are available for each of a number of businesses it is probably best to show the deviation of each business from the most successful business (in terms of the objective ratio). Figures 8.4 and 8.5 give an example of three companies drawn from the engineering case study of Chapter 5.

When the results are presented in the form suggested above and reviewed regularly by relevant management they facilitate the answering of such questions as: 'Return on capital has fallen by x per cent - Why?' 'Labour productivity has increased by x per cent - What has been its contribution to return on capital?' 'Plant A has been more successful than Plant B - Why?' The detail in which such questions can be answered will depend on the detail incorporated in the hierarchy.

The uses to which such analyses can be put is, however, the subject of Chapter 10. In the next chapter some of the pitfalls and problems most commonly encountered in establishing a performance measurement system are discussed.

Figure 8.4 : Company Comparison: Data

Company	A	B	C
Return on Capital %	28.7	9.4	12.6
Profit on Sales %	14.9	6.0	8.5
Sales/Capital	1.92	1.56	1.49

Figure 8.5 : Company Comparison: Presentation

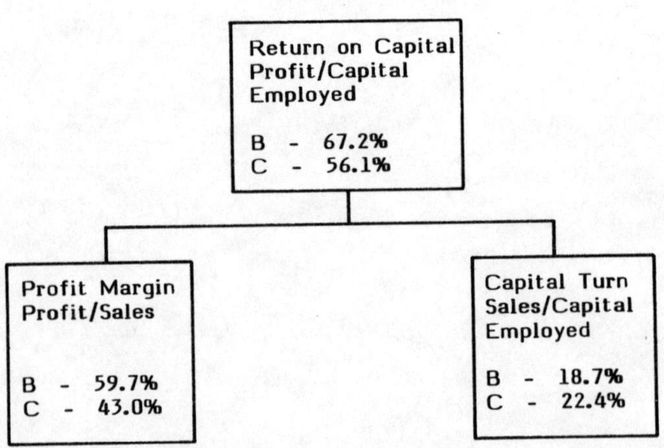

Figure 8.6 : Key Ratios

Return on Capital

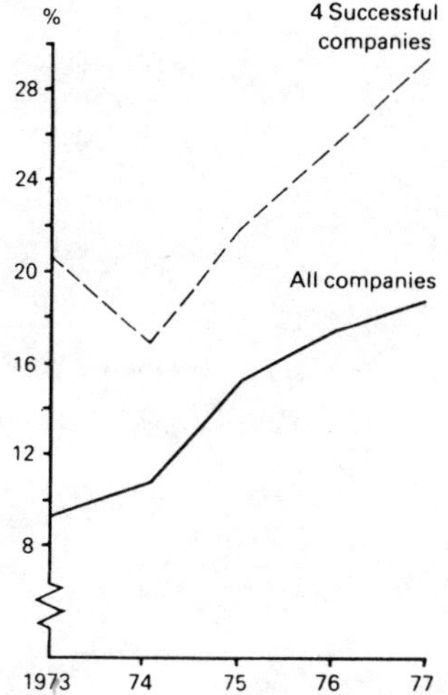

Profit Margin

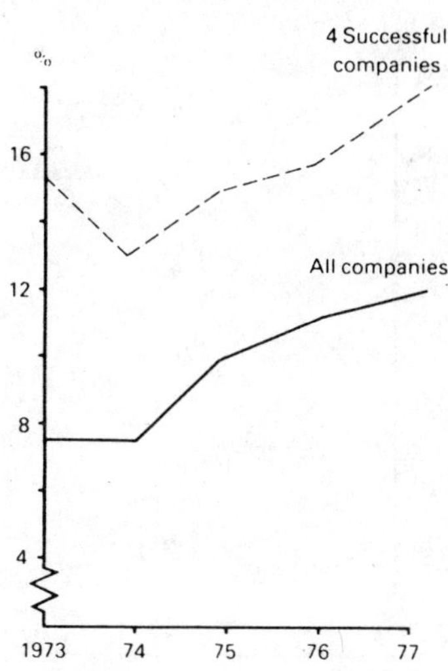

Sales: Capital Employed

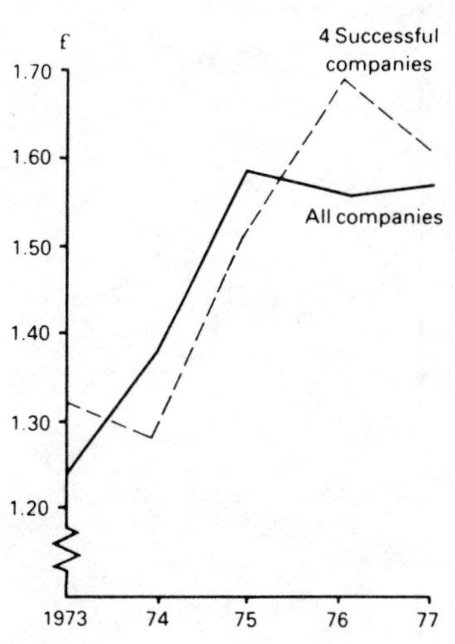

Profit: Gross Value Added

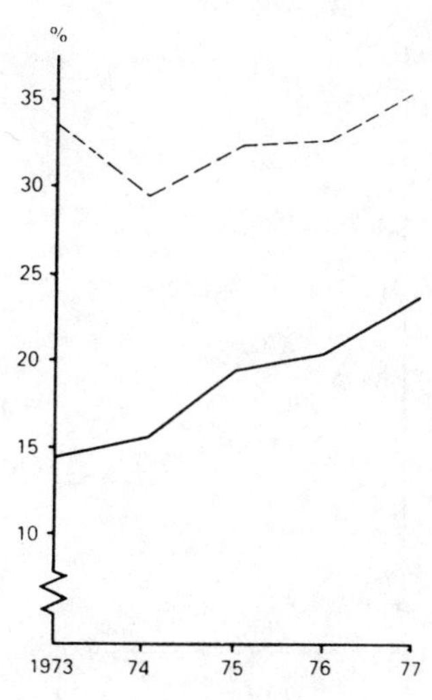

Figure 8.6 continued

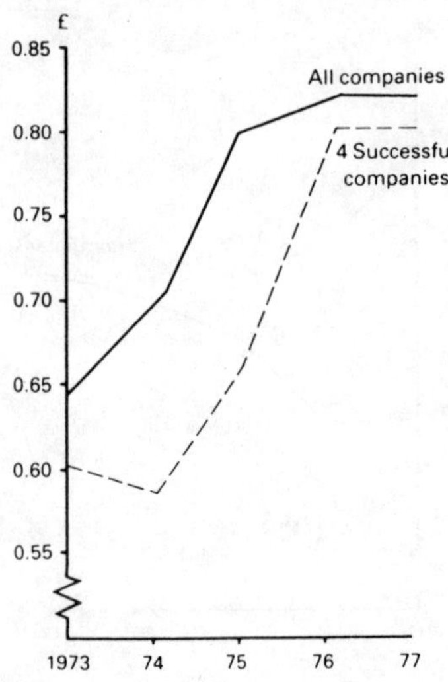

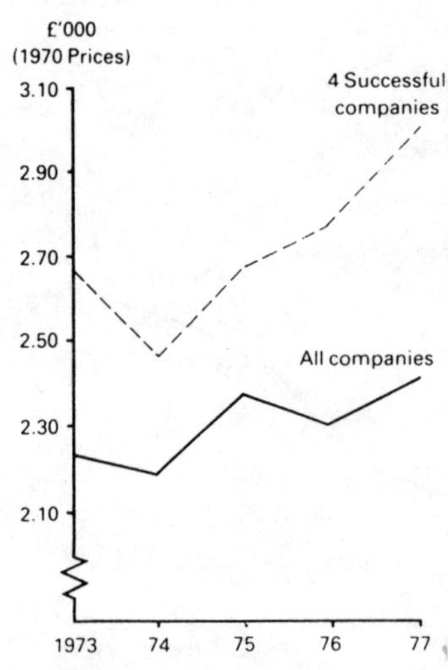

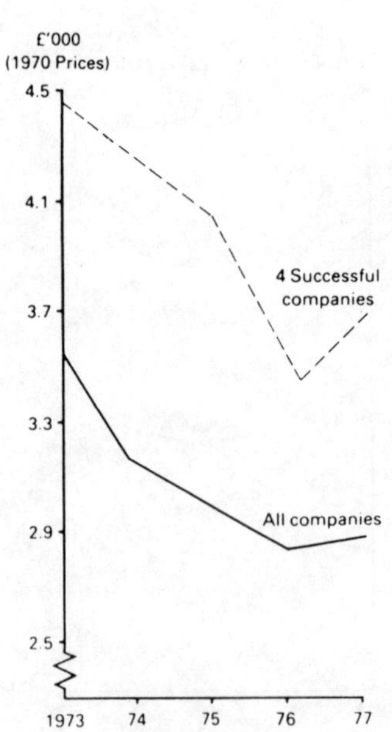

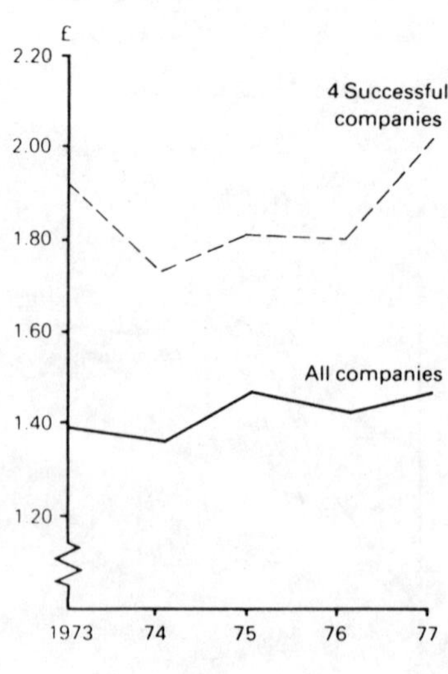

9 Problems of Performance Measurement

During the course of any project to establish a performance measurement system two types of problem will inevitably arise. The first type is the conceptual problem which often turns out to be one of definition. What is output? What are the important input factors? Which relationships are crucial to performance? Such problems are often quite daunting, even to an experienced practitioner, in setting up measurement systems and their solution lies in a clear and complete understanding of the business and the application to it of painstaking logical thought.

The other type of problem is the technical problem, which is often not exposed until the data collection stage is reached. What period of time should be selected? How should allocated items be treated? How can the effects of inflation be eliminated? Such problems may appear relatively trivial but their solution may require much tedious hard work and be crucial to achieving a sensible set of data and hence arriving ultimately at the correct set of ratios.

In this chapter some of the problems encountered in the case studies described and elsewhere under both headings will be discussed and, where possible, solutions indicated.

Conceptual Problems

(a) Defining Output

Some of the problems of defining output have been mentioned already in the case studies. However, in all those cases the problem was overcome by the use of a value or volume measure which was easily available and fairly readily acceptable as a valid measure. In two types of cases neither of these solutions is possible. The first is where output is difficult to define because of its sheer complexity; the second is where it is difficult to define because it is essentially qualitative and has only a minor, and possibly irrelevant, quantitative element.

The output of an insurance company is an example of the former type of problem. Insurance companies receive premia which they use to pay out claims and paid-up policies and to invest. Even leaving aside this last, which simply confuses the issue, output can hardly be regarded as the difference between premia and payments since this ignores the risk element associated with each policy, the existence of which necessitates an actuarial assessment of profit. It could also result in negative output!

The total value of premia is a misleading figure since many will be related to policies sold in previous years, while the number or value of new policies ignores the heavy input required to service existing ones. Clearly much of the work of many of the staff in insurance companies is routine and susceptible to clerical work measurement, but whilst such measures of output are suitable for measuring labour productivity they cannot be said to measure the output of the organisation as a whole since they are unrelated to its objectives. Insurance companies are in business to make profits, not to fill in forms and much form-filling may be done, very efficiently, without a penny of profit being earned.

Thus the measurement of output in an insurance company is a difficult problem. That is not to say it is insoluble but it is certainly not soluble in the same way as in the case studies presented in this book.

The second type of problem is that of largely qualitative, as opposed to quantitative, output. Examples might be a hospital ward, a personnel department, an R&D department. Clearly in all cases there will be some routine tasks which can be work-measured but the result will give no idea of the true output of the unit, since a large proportion of the work is non-routine and highly subjective in value. A nurse's work improves patient morale. A personnel officer's work improves employee morale. A scientist's work may bear no fruit but eliminates one more avenue to the ultimate goal.

Clearly, to measure output in such cases by means of those elements of the job which **can** be measured could produce very misleading results. It may be that in such cases output, and hence performance, cannot be measured. The 'good' nurse is the one who is known to be unfailingly encouraging, calm and considerate as well as efficient rather than the one who can make a bed most quickly or take the most temperatures in ten minutes. But even then opinions will vary since 'goodness' is subjective and perhaps there is no point in labouring too long to measure that which cannot be measured.

The problems of output definition and measurement could fill a book (but not this one). Many of the problems are more imaginary than real and it often, although not always, is a case of 'where there's a will there's a way'. Certainly, where a physical or financial output exists it should be the case that it can be satisfactorily defined.

(b) The Complexity Issue

The second conceptual problem of performance measurement is that of the sheer complexity of the model which emerges at the end of the analysis. The systems outlined in the transport and distribution case studies earlier are very complex and require considerable application before they will be understood and accepted as valid models. It is very easy, in the course of developing a model, to discourage those who are not fully committed to the need for such a model or who are simply too busy doing the job to put a great deal of effort into measuring it.

Sadly, many of the attempts to establish a measurement system which founder due to its increasing complexity fail, in fact, because of the lack of commitment of those concerned. Businesses are complex, particularly large ones making sophisticated products or providing extensive services. Hence any system which attempts to mirror the relationships within them will also be complex. If it is simple (like the engineering case study) it is because it is glossing over crucial details and is thus relatively useless as a basis for action.

In fact all the hierarchies presented in this book require an understanding of no more than the most basic algebra, ie

$$\frac{a}{b} = \frac{a}{c} \times \frac{c}{b}$$

and

$$\frac{a}{b} = \frac{a}{c} \div \frac{b}{c}$$

and equally basic arithmetic, ie

$$\text{if} \quad 2 + 3 + 5 = 10$$

$$\text{then} \quad \frac{2}{10} + \frac{3}{10} + \frac{5}{10} = \frac{10}{10} = 1$$

However, even simple algebra, when applied comprehensively to a complex system, can result in a bewildering mass of information. The more comprehensive the coverage of the measurement system, the more useful it becomes but the more complex it looks. It requires patience and application to understand the implications of even simple statements about complex situations; it is the absence of such qualities which often results in the rejection of systems as 'too complex'.

Technical Problems

(a) Data Collection

One of the most serious technical problems which arises in all attempts to measure performance to a greater or lesser extent is that of data collection. Very often the required data do not exist and it would be a great deal of work to collect them. This is obviously the case where, for instance, an output measure rests on clerical work measurement and no such system has been established. Similarly in manufacturing concerns standard labour hours measures are often available while standard material values are not.

Profit figures may not be available below a certain level of aggregation in a business or as frequently as they are ideally required and capital employed figures are notoriously difficult to obtain at anything below the highest level of aggregation.

Obviously problems of past data collection need not be repeated in the future and, since back data are only required to verify the model, such problems may be regarded as relatively trivial. However, models must be verified and it is a rare management which will agree to revised data collection methods to fit a model which cannot be proven on existing data. Clearly, however, this is the only path in some cases and hopefully one or at the most two years' data would be sufficient to validate the model.

(b) Cost Allocations

A related problem is encountered particularly in divisionalised companies where some costs, for instance head office costs, are allocated to the divisions on some arbitrary basis. Such a practice may not affect performance measurement but it will if the functions carried out by head office change over time or if the use made of head office services changes over time or varies from one division to another.

Normally such problems can be overcome by very careful analysis and, if necessary, reorganisation of the data but it can often be a tedious and time-consuming task.

(c) Periodicity

Another technical problem is the decision concerning the frequency with which the system will be measured. Two problems in particular arise. If performance is measured too frequently then the output of the period will not be related to the input of that period. An obvious example is the use of annual data for companies building ships or aeroplanes or power stations. Of course, if progress payments roughly keep pace with output then the problem may be solved; if they do not, then annual observations can give very strange results and a smoothing technique must be applied over the average job (ie order to delivery) length in order to provide meaningful ratios.

However, if performance is not measured frequently enough the results may be of no practical use. Annual data may be fine for long-term planning purposes but if performance levels go seriously awry in such a period, then for monitoring and corrective action purposes more frequent measures are needed. Unfortunately, more frequent measuring often results in statistical querks arising, such as seasonality, the unevenness of bonus payments, or random events, all of which are smoothed over in annual data. Such information therefore requires careful interpretation which again can be very time-consuming.

(d) Inflation

A final technical problem is that of the removal of inflation from financial data. Clearly time series which include inflation, ie measure values at current prices, are only meaningful if they are ratios relating one financial value to another which can reasonably be assumed to be inflating at the same rate. Profit on sales is probably a good example and, indeed, unless there is a very wide divergence in rates as there may have been in some companies during the 1970's in wage and price inflation, then ratios involving two value components do not need to be adjusted.

However, ratios such as sales per man clearly need to be adjusted as an increasing sales figure over time reflects both rising volume and prices.

During the engineering case study described in Chapter 5 a considerable amount of thought was given to this problem and many different solutions tried. The apparently most promising was to deflate each variable by the rate at which it had inflated over the period, according to the most appropriate published indices. Published indices are obviously, however, averages and the variables in the particular cases were unlikely to have risen at exactly that rate. In fact, the exercise produced results which were clearly nonsense.

It was eventually decided to deflate all financial series by the retail price index. Since there is no single index which will return all the series to their actual real values then the only justifiable course of action is to adjust all of them for changes in the purchasing power of money. Obviously, the lower the rate of inflation the less misleading such a procedure will be and it is in any case less misleading than any other except, of course, the case in which specific individual price indices for each variable have been collected by the unit concerned. If this had been done it would have been possible to deflate each series individually back to real values although the changes in relative real values over time revealed by use of a single index would then be lost.

Table 9.1 below gives an example of the deflation process.

Table 9.1 Removing Inflation from Financial Series

	Year 1	Year 2	Year 3
Sales - current prices	200	250	400
Actual price inflation index	75	80	100
Sales - real value	266.7	312.5	400
Retail Price Index	73	82	100
Sales - constant Year 3 prices	274	304.9	400

It is helpful, whichever index is used, to **reflate** earlier years to the latest years' prices rather than to **deflate** later years to the prices of an earlier one, simply because the resultant series is then expressed in prices which are currently meaningful. This does mean that each time a new observation is added the series has to be recalculated but this is a relatively small price to pay for the clear advantage of a series expressed in meaningful and familiar prices.

Conclusions

The experience of the case studies described earlier suggests that very few of the problems normally encountered in setting up a productivity measurement system are insurmountable, at least in those sectors and probably in many more. Whilst establishing such a system is rarely easy, and often involves much tedious data collection and analysis as well as concentrated participation by top management, the rewards gained, merely from the process of setting it up, are often quite significant in terms of enhanced appreciation of the problems of the business and potential barriers to their solution.

10 Potential Developments of the Performance Measurement Model

Throughout most of the earlier part of this book the performance measurement model has been described in terms of its 'problem analysis' role. It has been assumed that it will be used to monitor progress and thereby to analyse why performance is poor, the source of the problem, or perhaps why it has worsened or improved and the source of the change. A similar and related use has also been mentioned, when a unit is in a position to compare itself with another at the same point in time rather than with itself at a different point in time.

Both these uses, intrafirm (or intertemporal) and interfirm, are essentially backward-looking. They depend on back data and tell the unit something about what has been and possibly is still happening. They do not solve problems but rather define them.

But the ratio analysis method of business performance measurement is potentially a very powerful tool within the planning procedure and hence has a role as a problem-solving technique also. Since the method essentially provides a picture of the various relationships within the business it can be used as a basis for 'what if?' questions just as it can answer 'why?' questions. At the simplest level this can be done by adding a 'budget year' line to each result box to complement the results for the most recent year, last five years etc. In this way the impact of all budgeted changes can be assessed and implicit assumptions made explicit.

However, the hierarchy can be of use in the budgeting process itself. If the anticipated future values of all relevant variables expected to change over the period concerned are related to the most recent period's data, then the resultant ratios can be calculated and the expected impact of the changes assessed. A basis is thereby provided for planning any necessary action to improve the outlook or at least to avoid its worst consequences. For instance, figure 10.1 gives some basic data similar to the type produced in the engineering case study and then assumes that a rise in demand of 5 per cent and an increase in wages of 10 per cent may be expected. Figure 10.2 shows the predicted results.

Figure 10.1 Base Year Data and Expected Changes

	Base Year	Change	Result
Profit	40	derived from Value Added less Wages less Depreciation	33
Capital Employed	130	-	130
Sales	500	+5%	525
Value Added	410	Value Added: Sales ratio maintained	430.5
Numbers employed	25	-	25
Wages	275	+10%	302.5
Depreciation	95	-	95
Profit/Capital Employed	30.8	-17.5%	25.4
Profit/Sales	8.0	-21.4%	6.3
Sales/Capital Employed	3.8	+ 5.0%	4.0
Profit/Value Added	9.8	-21.4%	7.7
Value Added/Capital Employed	3.2	+ 5.0%	3.3
Value Added/Men	16.4	+ 5.0%	17.2
Capital Employed/Men	5.2	-	5.2
Value Added/Wages	1.5	- 4.5	1.4
Wages/Men	11.0	+10.0%	12.1

Obviously, assumptions have to be made concerning the relationship between sales and value added and levels of capital employed, depreciation and the labour force. Figure 10.2 assumes no change in any of these variables and predicts that if the expected changes take place, return on capital will fall by 17.5 per cent to 25.4 per cent. If this is not a high enough return, then the required (for example) reduction in the labour force/increase in labour productivity to prevent the fall can be calculated.

Obviously, the example quoted is very simple and hardly merits a productivity model. However, once several simultaneous changes are anticipated, the model provides a useful framework for ordering the calculations, making explicit the assumptions required and ensuring consistency. It is even more essential to have such a framework, however, if future changes can only be predicted with relative uncertainty and some assessment of the risk facing future results is required. The productivity ratio approach can be used to assess the risk involved in future changes of uncertain magnitude with the use of a technique known as

Figure 10.2 : Expected Value Predictions

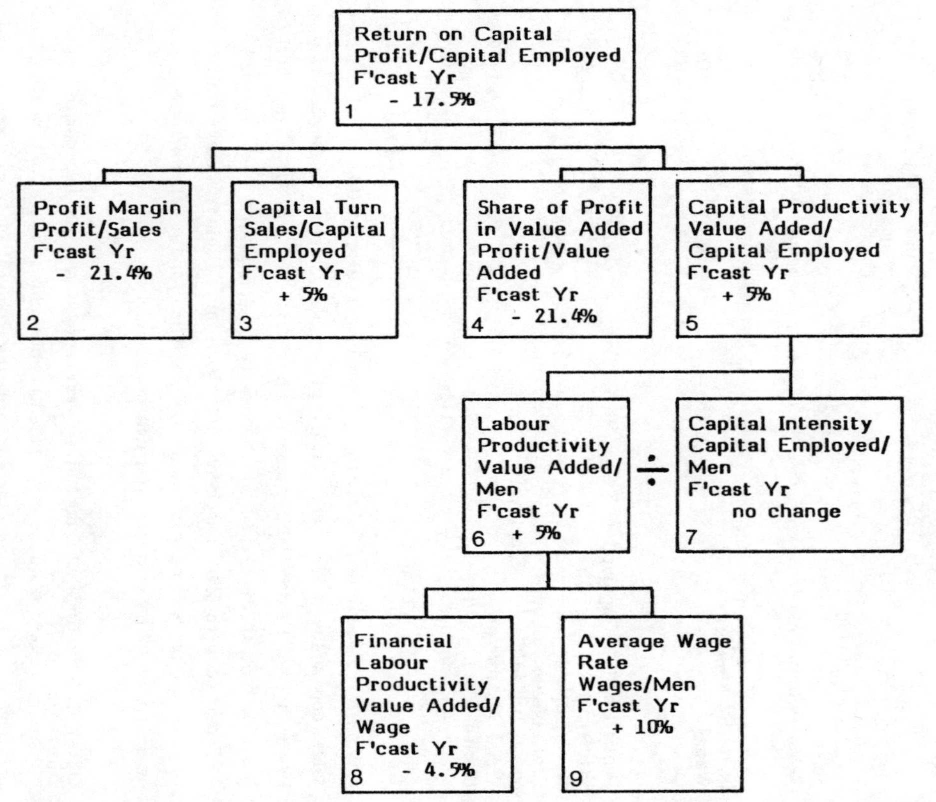

'risk simulation'.

Taking figure 10.1 as a base once again it is assumed that it is still expected that demand will rise by 5 per cent and wages by 10 per cent. However, in this case less certainty exists. Sales might actually fall by as much as 10 per cent or could rise by up to 20 per cent. Similarly, wages could be held to a 3 per cent increase or could go up by as much as 15 per cent. Given such uncertainty, how can the expected level of return on capital be calculated and what is the risk of, for example, making a return of below 20 per cent?

Using the technique known as 'risk simulation', distributions of the variables expected to change are used rather than expected values only and a very large number of 'runs' of the model is carried out. On each occasion one possible outcome for each variable is selected and all the resultant ratios calculated. On average, the expected value will still be selected, of course, but extreme values will also be selected as often as the distribution allows. If the distribution gives wages a 10 per cent chance of increasing by more than 12 per cent, then in 10 per cent of the 'runs' a value greater than 12 per cent will be selected.

In figure 10.3 the chance of a return on capital of below 20 per cent is given by the shaded area as a percentage of the total; the chance of a loss by the hatched area, and so on. Thus, while the expected outcome is one which could have been calculated simply, the additional information input provides a much more sensitive, and hence useful, outcome.

Clearly the results of such an exercise will only be as good as the information provided. Clearly also, a computer program is necessary, not because the technique is particularly complex but simply to cope with the very large number of calculations involved.

This description of the use of risk simulation in association with ratio analysis has been necessarily brief; more detailed exposition of the 'risk simulation' technique can be found in the text cited earlier[1] (Chapter 8).

Figure 10.3 : Distribution of Return on Capital Using Risk Simulation

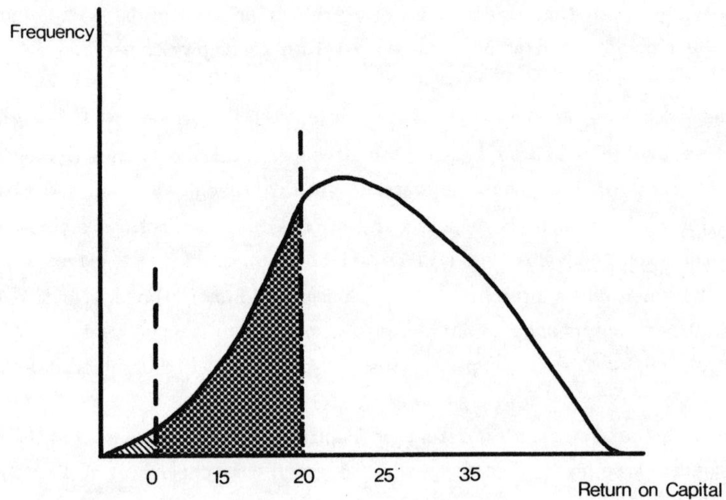

The technique described above is a potentially most powerful planning tool combining as it does accuracy in mirroring the relationships governing the performance of the firm and sensitivity in dealing with uncertain future events. Unusually for such a powerful tool it is also essentially simple; the hardest part of using a performance measurement hierarchy to plan the future is building the hierarchy in the first place.

11 Conclusion

The reader of this book should now be in a position to tackle the problem of measuring the performance of his business. He should return to Chapter 3, work through Steps 1-6 as listed in the Annex and then construct his hierarchy using Rules 1-4 together with Rules 5-7 from Chapter 6 if he is in a divisionalised company.

Several heads are likely to be better than one in putting together an initial hierarchy, looking at past data, revising the ratios and agreeing a set for regular use. An independent, 'outside' head can be particularly useful since a key ingredient for success is an unbiased view of the factors which really are crucial to the success of the business. But no outsider can do the whole job; no outsider can have the understanding of the individual business necessary to get it right. The ideal team is an internal one with external help.

It is vital not to be daunted by practical problems or apparent complexities. Some benefit will be gained simply by **trying** to measure performance and with the aid of this book at least some of the problems and complexities may disappear.

Index